Will I be Called
an Author?

By the same author

The Glasgow Gospel
A Scots Gospel
Auld Testament Tales
A Glasgow Bible

Will I be Called an Author?

Jamie Stuart

LINDSAY PUBLICATIONS

First Published in 2000 by
Lindsay Publications
Glasgow

ISBN 1 898169 17 9

A CIP record of this book is available from the British Library

Designed and typeset in 11/13pt Caslon
by Creative Imprint, Glasgow

Front cover illustration by John Gahagan

Printed and bound in Finland by Werner Söderström, Osakeyhtiö

❁ ❁ ❁

Contents

To
Shona and Gillian

ACKNOWLEDGEMENTS

The author would like to express his sincere thanks to the following for their help in the preparation of this book: Mary McCleod, Ken Colville, Jeremy Goh, Les McGregor and Dr Donald Smith. Gratitude is particularly extended to my daughters Elizabeth and Fiona and to my granddaughter Kirsty for their encouragement, contributions, typing and tolerance. I am grateful to Jim Simpson for his line illustrations and Brian J Dunabie of BJD Photographics for the cover photograph.

My appreciation to Ranald MacColl for kind permission to include the Lobey Dosser Sketch.

To the *Citizens' Theatre* for years of joy and pleasure and for allowing me to reprint the Mauler Macrae script.

Sources

The British Airman,
Roger A Freeman, Arms and Armour, 1989

Bounce the Rhine,
Charles Whiting, Grafton Books

Travelling Hopefully,
Helen Murdoch, Paul Harris Publishing

Wise Enough to Play the Fool,
Pricilla Barlow, John Donald Limited

The Pageant of the Century,
Oldhams Press Limited

FOREWORD

THIS IS A STORY OF Glasgow through the twentieth century. Decade by decade it bears witness to the city's people and to the ever-changing backdrop of history.

But rising above the history is the spirit of Glasgow and in particular of a talented lad whose story spans the First World War to the new millennium.

This lad Jimmy Stuart – wee Ginger or now Jamie – has talent and a bit of get-up-and-go. He has no special privileges, he has to take his knocks with the rest and some of them are 'sair dunts'. Yet every time he picks himself up and has another go. Is this not the story of Glasgow?

There is a restlessness here as well. Jamie Stuart could claim to have seven lives. He has been an athlete, actor, airman, salesman, social worker, author and evangelist. For Jamie there is always a new challenge, another hill to climb even if nowadays it is with the help of two skilfully replaced knees!

It could have been a disaster – at several points it almost was – but two things have given Jamie Stuart the will to keep going. One is his sense of humour, evident throughout these pages. In Jamie's hands even the Bible can be a source of fun and laughter as his best-selling *The Glasgow Gospel* shows.

The other thing, underpinning all, is his Christian faith and commitment. At key moments in this story you find Jamie Stuart turning to God, not as a distant idea but as a present help and support. Thousands of ordinary Glaswegians will testify to that.

I appear late in his story because the enthusiasms of a young theatre director and an aspirant author sparked off each other, to put Jamie's *A Scots Gospel* on stage, on tour and in print. It has been a privilege and an inspiration to work with this wee man – but don't let on I told you. Glasgow Jamie is truly a Glasgow witness.

DR DONALD SMITH
Director, The Netherbow Theatre
Edinburgh

EARLY DAYS

THE MIDWIFE SMILED. My wee naked body was safely delivered into her eager hands. There had been no stress – but yes, some blood, sweat and tears. Let me tell you about the tears.

The date was 10 September, 1920. I had two brothers – John and Peter – six years and three years old respectively. My mother had always been desperate for a girl and hoped fervently that the good Lord would answer her prayer. Surely number three would meet her heart's desire?

'Well now, Mrs Stuart,' said the midwife, 'you can have a shot now, there you are, lassie – a lovely big boy!' Hear this! My mother burst into tears and wept uncontrollably for several minutes.

Dr McNab came forward. 'Dear me! Dear me! What's all this carry-on about, Mrs Stuart? What's vexing you?'

'I'm fine, Doctor,' my mother replied, blowing her nose furiously, 'but you see, I wanted a wee girl this time.' And the wailing increased in volume.

'Mrs Stuart,'said the Doc, 'you should be ashamed of yourself. We've had no trouble at all; you have at your bosom a lovely healthy boy. He looks great. I'll tell you this – you are the mother of a Prize Baby!'

In later years, my mother, bless her heart, in a kind of way lived to regret telling me the story of my entry into the world. Whenever she had cause to reprimand me for any reason, I would remind her that I was her Prize Baby! This usually prompted a smart scud in the rear end, and I would get the message! (By the way, the last addition to the family was also a boy!)

Fortunately for me the message I received in childhood was one of love and devotion from committed Christian parents. My father was born in Tobermory on the Isle of Mull and arrived in Glasgow as a 14-year-old with his widowed mother. My mother was born in Glasgow's Gorbals and married my father in 1913. Born in 1920, I completed the 'Trio of Apostles', Peter, James and John. Three years later Ronald was born; I can't remember why he wasn't christened Andrew. My birthplace was number 48 Kingarth Street in the Crosshill district of Glasgow, very near the centre of the city, but I have virtually no memory of my first five years living there.

In 1925 things were looking up for my dad. He was in full charge of the warehouse of Thomson and Mathieson Ltd, fruit brokers, merchants and importers at 40 Ingram Street, Glasgow and had been employed with the firm for twelve years. He reckoned that his job was secure and had managed to save a bit of money. Leaving the city, he took his wife and four boys into the country – into a pleasant village called Stepps, just ten miles away. The address was MarieVille, Alexandra Avenue; our bungalow was situated at the foot of the Avenue. We had a huge garden and an unrestricted view of the countryside. Life was good. John Stuart from Tobermory had made it! He created a lovely garden filled with an array of trees, shrubs and heathers. At the back we had all kinds of vegetables plus two white rabbits and a dozen hens, so there was no shortage of freshly laid eggs. Along with my brothers, Jack and Peter, I attended the local primary school just ten minutes away via the short cut past the tennis courts. On Sundays, Mum and Dad marched proudly to the Church of Scotland in Blenheim Avenue with their four sons.

At the bottom of our avenue, the Girl Guides had a small wooden hut. It was situated in a field directly across from our house and I can well remember being spellbound when seeing my first ever concert in that place. To a seven-year-old it was magic indeed – accordions, fiddles, dancing, singing and recitations. The atmosphere must have had an effect on me;

in later years I spent some years as a thespian 'treading the boards.' Interestingly enough, about 150 yards from the Guides' Hut (it's still there) is the Parish Church of Stepps. In January 1999, I was invited to their annual Burns' Supper to recite 'Holy Willie's Prayer'and 'Tam O'Shanter.' Memories of the Guides' concert seventy years before kept drifting back.

In the summer we explored 'The Wee Wood' and the North Woods. The local farmer allowed us to ride on the hay-carts at harvest time. My brothers and I enjoyed good health and I think we were reasonably well behaved, although I do recall a time when we raised the ire of my dad. The four of us shared a room and one night (about midnight) we engaged in a very competitive pillow fight. It would appear that it got out of control, because I remember my dad turfing the four of us out of the house in our pyjamas, onto the cold, wet grass until we cooled down.

For holidays, Dad bought a big tent and we went camping to Balmaha on the Banks of Loch Lomond. We scaled Ben Lomond, stayed to see the sunrise and felt on top of the world.

My mother was a small lady, five feet and one inch tall. We all loved her dearly, and why not? She was the most gentle and caring of people and I honestly cannot remember her losing her temper, although with four energetic sons I'm sure she must have had cause. Anyway I remember her as a kindly mother and an able parent. She played the piano and sang sweetly, was a super cook and a good baker. Her smile was pure gold; she laughed a lot and enjoyed reading Annie S Swan in *The People's Friend*. Our family was blessed with two caring and disciplined parents who led by example. Dad earned £5 per week in 1926, which I guess would have been an above average wage. He was a gifted handyman and personally made the beds we slept in. He also equipped himself with shoemaker's tools and repaired the footwear for all six of the family. We didn't go into Glasgow City Centre very much as a family, but I have a memory of visiting a

Pantomime at the Princess' Theatre in the Gorbals (now the Citizens' Theatre) and seeing the popular comedian George West in a show. It was great value in those days, the panto-mimes lasted for four hours! I remember my parents taking us to the Green's Cinema in Renfield Street (at that time the biggest cinema in Europe) and seeing Charles Laughton and Norma Shearer in *The Barretts of Wimpole Street*. I also have a glimmer of a memory of being taken to Hengler's Circus in Sauchiehall Street (the ABC Cinemas are now located there). The great comedy attraction was Doodles the Clown who always seemed to get wrapped up in the carpet. Also there was a most spectacular water scene, which of course flabber-gasted the children present.

On 26 October 1926, my father suffered a cruel blow, one from which he never fully recovered. On that day, as he left work he was given a letter:

Dear John,

I regret that we are unable to keep you on in our employ-ment at the wage you are receiving and we would prefer if you would look out for another situation commencing Monday 8 November.

If you would rather stay on here it could only be at a weekly wage of £2 10s.

Yours faithfully

JH THOMSON.

Dad was obliged to seek another job. On 12 November, he received a reference from Thomson and Mathieson Ltd:

TO WHOM IT MAY CONCERN

The bearer, Mr John Stuart, was in our employment for a period of about twelve years. He acted at first as a Dispatch Clerk to our Travellers' Department, and latterly he was in full charge of our Warehouse. In both these positions we found him to be thoroughly reliable and trustworthy, and we have pleasure in recommending him to anyone who requires an efficient and competent warehouseman.

Yours truly,

ROBT. R ALLAN

Managing Director

The story goes that dad's employer wanted to place a family member in Dad's position and so my honest, hard-working father was sacrificed. In later years, he confided in me, 'James, I sat with my head in my hands in George Square and wondered what on earth I was going to do!'

It must be realised that in 1926 the economy was not buoyant and a depression was imminent. In May of that year the Trade Unions empowered the General Council of the TUC to call a National Strike, to support the miners. They had been locked out by the mine-owners after refusing to accept wage cuts and changed conditions. A mile from our house, across the fields, soldiers with fixed bayonets stood guard at the pit-head of Cardowan Colliery. Transport workers, railwaymen, dockers, printers and industrial workers throughout the country stopped work. There were no newspapers. Industry was paralysed and the Government refused to move. The strike lasted for nine days. The Wall Street Stock Exchange crash of 1929 produced world-wide misery and triggered what was called The Great Depression which lasted until the mid 1930s. This was a period of low output and investment with high unemployment. Times were bad in the UK; in the USA they were a disaster!

During 1932, the worst year of the depression, thirty-four million Americans were without any income. Thousands of people, unable to find even a soup kitchen, rummaged for food among the garbage. In country districts they ate weeds. A popular song of that time was 'Buddy, can you spare a dime?' about a man who had helped to build the American dream and now found himself begging in the street. My dad hired a horse and cart, bought fruit and vegetables from the market, and for the next five months tried to make a living selling his produce round the streets of Stepps. Unfortunately, he wasn't cut out to be an outside trader and often ended up giving his stock away for nothing rather than dumping it. On 13 April 1927, he was employed as an agent with the Scottish Legal Life Assurance Society and remained with that Society until his retirement in 1949, aged sixty-five.

In 1929 we couldn't afford to remain in Stepps and were obliged to move. It must have been a traumatic time for my folks but at nine years of age the reality of the situation did not affect me. I trusted my parents implicitly and felt that all would turn out well. We packed up our goods and chattels and settled in Carntyne in the East End of Glasgow, in a four-in-a-block Council house in Carntyne Road. A few years later we moved to a semi-detached house in Edinburgh Road, Carntyne, once more with our own gate and large garden.

⊛ ⊛ ⊛

BIBLE EXAM

⊛ ⊛ ⊛

I AM STILL LIVING IN THIS HOUSE and attend High Carntyne Parish Church, just around the corner. I'm an Elder in the Kirk and also the Prayer Secretary. The Church came into being in 1930, in a large wooden hut that was the property of the 162nd Boys' Brigade Company. The Reverend Robert Kirkland conducted the first Service of Worship on Sunday 30 March, 1930. More than twenty people attended and we have a record of the offering at that historic service – £1.13s.9d. (£1.70) On hearing about a Sunday School for young folk attached to High Carntyne Church I enrolled immediately, as I didn't want to repeat the embarrassment I had suffered one year earlier in Stepps Village Church. Here's the story of that episode in my young life.

I expect that most of us want to be good at something – to be an achiever. Success in one's life and in general relationships is surely a common goal. My earliest recollection of attempting success (and winning a prize!) in an exam was a disaster. Each Sunday that God sent I had to satisfy my mum and dad that the back of my neck and ears were scrubbed, my ginger hair was slicked down and my boots were well polished. The bells were ringing; Mr and Mrs Stuart and family made their way to the Kirk.

For some reason or other I was not a member of the Sunday School. I've no doubt my parents were busy enough coping with life in those hard times. Our only connection with the Church was the Sunday morning service and I didn't think to question my parents about Sunday School. Church attendance was a great joy for me. I loved the atmosphere and the dignity of all concerned. The sermons were long and I certainly didn't understand them but my attention was alerted one year when the Sunday School Bible Exam prizes were presented. I decided that I too would be fair proud to step up to the front of the Kirk and receive a prize. The following Spring a pulpit intimation was read out stating that the Bible exams would be held in the church hall on the first Saturday of the next month at three pm. I was eight years old. I desperately wanted to win a prize and to shake hands with the minister's wife.

The important day arrived and I reported at the church hall. The teachers seemed surprised to see me. Who could blame them? I wasn't a member of the Sunday School and had not received even a vestige of instruction or preparation to equip me for the test. Even so, I was directed to a desk, upon which lay several sheets of white paper, a pen and a pot of ink. At one minute to three the question paper was handed out and at three o'clock sharp the bell was rung. My first action was dead easy. I wrote my name and age at the top of the first sheet. I read the first question and realised I couldn't answer it; likewise the second question, and the third, and so on to the end of the paper. I was totally out of my depth. I knew nothing. The other boys and girls were writing away furiously. I blew my nose for something to do. My face was hot. I could feel it burning. My head was bursting. I was in agony. The tears splashed onto the virgin paper – well, not quite – it had my name and age on it.

A teacher noticed my torment and quietly asked if I was not well. I mimed to her that I had a headache and, without making eye contact with anyone, I tip-toed to the door. Outside I breathed the fresh air of an escaped prisoner. My mum and dad knew nothing of my doings and I never informed a living soul about that sorry day.

CARNTYNE

ARRIVING IN CARNTYNE IN 1929, I seemed to make the transition from the rural atmosphere of Stepps to the outskirts of the big city of Glasgow with the greatest of ease. Along with my pals I went on the rowing boats at Hogganfield Loch and played pitch and putt and golf at Lethamhill Golf Course. I joined everything – the swimming baths, the library, the dramatic societies and the junior choir. I wasn't particularly interested in girls, but I do remember noting that there was a certain choir member called May Kelt who was most attractive.

We climbed trees and played cricket. There weren't many cars or buses around at that time and I recall that we played football in the middle of Carntyne Road – on home-made stilts! I went through the various departments of our Church Sunday School – Primary, Junior, Intermediate and Senior, plus the Junior and Senior Bible Classes. In the early thirties Carntyne was a burgeoning housing scheme containing many families. High Carntyne Church boasted the largest Sunday School in Scotland – 1000 pupils and 100 teachers.

The church was the hub of the community and its minister the Reverend Tom Crichton was the life and soul of the church. His ministry began in 1930 and lasted until 1948. He was a World War I veteran, having lost a leg in the conflict. However, his disability did not affect his ministry and he made good use of his Baby Austin car to get around the parish.

The annual Sunday School summer trip was a big occasion in the lives of the young folk. In the early thirties we did not travel to the location by bus or train, probably because of the cost involved. Lorries were borrowed from the local farmer or coalman. Clydesdale horse-power was used and the animals were dressed up to the nines – gleaming brass ornaments on their harnesses and the most colourful and elaborate decorations on their tails. They were equine wonders to behold. Banners, flags, balloons and streamers disguised the lorries. The girls wore pretty dresses and ribbons in their hair. The boys wore white shirts and white sannies (plimsolls). In those days we didn't travel very far; usually to a large field a few miles away from the church, with enough space to run the races and play five-a-side football. Margaret Smith, former Session Clerk of the Kirk, has a vivid memory of one of the early summer trips. Arriving at the chosen field, our eager Margaret started to run and slipped, in her white dress, full length, onto a large cowpat. Ever ready to accept the challenge, Mr Crichton helped Margaret into his car and drove the few miles back to Carntyne. Mrs Smith got the lass into a bath and into another dress and they drove back to the fun and games.

Sunday School parties at Christmas were always happy occasions although one of the Junior Department's regular games was of doubtful popularity. Many of the boys hid in the toilets when Bee Baw Babbity was announced. Silly boys! I was all for it – a kissing game. The teachers would round up as many lads and lassies who were willing and circles were formed with everyone holding hands. A boy would be placed in the centre of the circle. The pianist then struck up the tune and we moved clockwise singing 'Bee Baw Babbity, Babbity, Babbity, Bee Baw Babbity, kiss a bonny wee lassie.' At this point the boy would select a girl, give her a peck and the girl would then go into the centre – and so on. It was very daring, and my first memory of a collision with a girl's lips. Rena Morgan was in the centre of the ring and on cue, chose me for a cheeper. She was a pretty girl. Seventy years on, we keep in touch and she's still a cracker.

I worked hard at my preparation for Bible exams and began

a hobby of aiming for prizes. I joined the Life Boys and in due course was promoted to the Boys' Brigade. My memories of service with the 162nd Company of the Boys' Brigade are bittersweet. Certainly – in the main – I give thanks for the Christian fellowship I enjoyed, for learning the importance of discipline, for the athletic training and for all the fun and games. I earned the major award of the Boys' Brigade – the King's Badge – and was fair proud to wear it on my arm. As a 14 year-old I won the Glasgow Battalion Mile Championship, and was looking forward to defending my title when an upset happened in my BB career. Looking back on the incident, I can smile, but I must have been a sorry lad at the time. Ye see I told a wee lie! Well that's not quite accurate. It wisnae a wee lie. It was a gey big lie!

One Friday evening I requested to be excused from Drill Squad, complaining of a sprained ankle. I was really all right, and the following day won a three-mile cross-country race. Next Friday however , a shock awaited me. Over one hundred boys were standing in the ranks. *Without any previous warning to me, without any meeting, or hint of any kind,* the Captain of the Company made the following announcement: 'Now boys, I have something serious to say. Last week one of our boys told a lie, and I'm sorry to say that the person involved is one of our best lads.' I was a Corporal at the time and was staggered by what followed.

'The boy I refer to is Corporal James Stuart. As punishment he will lose his stripes and return to the ranks.'

Certainly I deserved to be reprimanded – but to be reduced to the ranks? I felt cheated and I've no regrets about my response. Without any hesitation I marched smartly down the hall, up onto the platform, removed my belt and my lanyard and deposited them on the Captain's table. 'Sir, I resign from the Company,' I said and walked off home. I was not contacted and of course lost my mile title since I could not defend it.

It's a funny old world isn't it? And ironic that I'm now invited to be Guest of Honour at Boys' Brigade inspections and to adjudicate their Bible exams.

I completed my primary school education at Riddrie School, passed my qualifying exam and went to Whitehill Secondary School. Alas, my Secondary School education did not win me any prizes. I could make my excuses: each morning I was up at 6 a.m. doing a paper round and in the evenings I neglected my homework for training with Carntyne Amateur Athletics Club. As a result of these activities I often fell asleep in class. As a member of the school Drama Club I remember performing in the City Hall and I also ran well in the annual sports meetings, but as a student I was not a success. In fact I was obliged to repeat my second year of studies and left school at fifteen. My father thought it was a good idea and I didn't argue with him.

GOING TO THE DOGS

MY FIRST JOB was AS AN OFFICE BOY at a flour and grain merchant's office – John Richmond Ltd in McAlpine Street near Anderston Cross. I hated it. The chief clerk bullied me and I determined on the first day that I would give it a trial but vowed there and then that I would not remain for more than one year.

As the deadline date drew near I applied for a position as a salesman in Charles Rattray and Co, the well-known wholesale warehouse in Candleriggs. My interview was successful and I was assigned to the blanket department – at a pay of thirty shillings (£1.50) per week. In John Richmond's I had been earning ten shillings (50p) per week. I felt like a millionaire! I was fair pleased to give in my notice at John Richmond Ltd. The boss informed me that he had actually been considering giving me a rise in my pay and that he was sorry to lose me. His name was Mr Gibson. The clerk and I nicknamed him Hoot Gibson after the popular cowboy actor in the Hollywood films of that time. Come to think of it – Mr Gibson was a cowboy right enough!

My mum was delighted for me. She would take the pound note and I would keep the ten shillings for pocket money. Life was good. In fact, so good that one night I nearly 'went to the dogs' both literally and metaphorically. Let me explain. Some of my pals were keen to sample the thrills of gambling at Carntyne Greyhound Stadium, one mile from where I lived and I went along with them. The stadium had recently opened and was one of the first to be built in the city. It was a novelty for the Glasgow gamblers and they flocked to it like bees to a honey-pot. In fact the stadium owners were so keen to keep the customers dry on wet days that they erected a covered walkway about half a mile long which stretched from the tram car stop in Duke Street and led right up to the turnstile entrance. There were programme sellers, bookies, tipsters, tick-tack men and hot pie stalls. The meeting started at 6pm on a Friday – pay day. In possession of my envelope containing my precious thirty shillings and, straight from work, I joined my friends knowing that I had ten shillings to stake. After six races I had lost the lot. I was not a happy wee boy. I thought of George Raft, the Hollywood film star who always seemed to be losing thousands of dollars in the gambling casinos. A gambler always wants to recoup his losses. I took a mad risk. I staked ten shillings of my mum's pay in race seven. No luck! I could almost feel my father's heavy hand on the back of my head and on my backside.

There was one race left. Six dogs were on view. The race favourite was the Scottish greyhound champion, by the name of Ballycurreen Soldier. In my opinion, this dog could not lose. He was a lovely animal and very popular. The odds were 2 to 1. Nervously I went to the betting window. I surrendered the rest of my mother's cash on the counter. 'Ten shillings on *Ballycureen Soldier* to win,' I whispered. There was a lot of running and shouting as last bets were placed. The tote windows were slammed shut as the six healthy, eager greyhounds were led into the traps. The punters crossed their fingers as the stadium lights were switched off and searchlights lit up the track. The bell rang and the backers bellowed. The electric hare wheeched off and by jings, Ballycureen Soldier wheeched off in hot pursuit. He romped home the winner by five lengths. Wee Jimmy went home with his thirty bob back in his pocket. It was a salutary lesson – nearly 'going to the dogs.'

I worked for two years with Rattray's and then moved into Gent's Outfitting. The shop at the corner of Buchanan Street and St Vincent Street has been a Gents' store for as long as

I can remember. In 1939 it was Watsons Ltd, and my boss was Mr Sam Vickery. He was a tall, strapping, smart gentleman in a check suit, bright waistcoat, bow tie and with a curly moustache. He dined at Danny Brown's just round the corner in St Vincent Street.

Danny Brown's Restaurant is no more, but in 1940 it was one of the most prestigious eateries in the city, frequented by prosperous business people. Sam Vickery rubbed shoulders with bankers, lawyers and entrepreneurs. It was a 'place to be seen', and Mr V seemed expert in being chummy and passing round cigars. Needless to say, patrons of Danny Brown's often called at Watson's Ltd to purchase top of the range shirts and suits at the top market prices.

In the early part of 1940, a dozen Polish seamen rolled into the shop. Their ship had been sunk and a British vessel had rescued them. After having disembarked at Greenock they made their way to what was probably an office of the exiled Polish government in Glasgow and, armed with a wad of notes, arrived in Buchanan Street on a freezing cold day.

They wore makeshift attire and were in need of warm overcoats. Only one of them spoke a little English. They were extremely subdued, friendly and very courteous. The spokesman proudly introduced himself to me with a name something like Vladek Bienkovsky. I think he was the Captain. 'We want to buy big coats,' he smiled. 'Today in Glasgow it is – how you say? Bloody cold!' I agreed with him about the weather and took the crew below decks, leaving the junior assistant to man the reception area. The boss had just left for Danny Brown's.

We had a large stock of winter overcoats, so it was easy for me to fit out all the sailors. However, there was great merriment as I struggled to find one for a large sailor (probably the ship's cook) who must have weighed about seventeen stones. An outsize Crombie coat soon covered his massive frame and he strutted about like a model to great applause from his mates. I noted all the prices on one receipt and Mr Vladek paid the bill. Upstairs, each man ceremoniously shook my hand as he left the shop. I had secured my biggest sale ever and wished them plain sailing.

Stuffing the crisp new notes into the till, I eagerly awaited the return of my employer. Having had his roast beef and a glass or two of wine, Mr V breezed in. He always made straight for the till to check the sales. His eyes popped. I got a bonus and the rest of the afternoon off.

MOLLY URQUHART

❀❀❀

I THINK REALLY, that the acting bug first bit me when, as a nine year-old, I was cast in a short play produced by the Life Boys (the junior section of the Boys' Brigade.) I only had half a dozen lines to spout but I remember making the most of them. I still have the script. From then on I joined every amateur dramatic club that I could find; my own church club, various other church drama clubs, the Boys' Brigade concert party, the Whitehill School Society and the Lyric Players based in the YMCA in Sauchiehall Street.

Then it happened. I met Molly Urquhart! For an ambitious young would-be actor it was a golden opportunity. Born and brought up in Glasgow, Molly decided not only to be an actress but also to establish her own theatre. She accomplished both of these aims triumphantly. As an actress, she was one of the stalwarts of the Glasgow Citizens' Theatre, made television appearances in *Doctor Finlay's Casebook*, and went on to become internationally successful as a film actress.

In 1939, aged thirty-three, Molly founded her own theatre in an old church hall in Rutherglen, and christened it the MSU Theatre, after her own initials. It was later to become the Rutherglen Repertory Theatre.

So it was that in August 1940, at nineteen, I got the chance I had been waiting for. Coming home from work on the bus one night, I read about the MSU in Mamie Crichton's Theatre Column in the *Glasgow Evening News*. Hotfooting it the same night to Main Street, Rutherglen, I bowled into the theatre. Rehearsal was in progress and at the first break,

27

Molly herself came down to speak to me.

'Good evening.' I smiled hopefully, 'My name's James Stuart. I'm from Carntyne. I've just been reading in tonight's *Evening News* about your company and I wonder if I could have an audition?'

'Well, you've got a famous name, young man. The big chap in Hollywood's done well for himself.' She put her arm round my shoulder and walked me down to the stage. 'Now, James Stuart, it just happens that I need one more actor to complete my cast for the particular play that we've started rehearsing. This is James Stuart, folks,' she announced to the players on the stage. 'Right, James.' Molly handed me a script. 'Your character is Mr Blow. You appear on page three. You're a loud-mouthed reporter, so belt it out, son.' It was a great wee part. I belted it out and that was my baptism into the MSU.

My time with Molly's 'Good Companions' lasted for one whole season, and I appeared in every production. On reflection, I realise that I was involved in what was probably the most unique theatrical venture ever undertaken in the UK.

The MSU existed for four years – the worst years of World War II – under the leadership of Molly Urquhart. The company consisted of twelve regular members. Nearly all of them held down jobs during the day. They were teachers, office workers, sales people, printers, bankers and the like. It was classed as a semi-professional theatre company. By that I mean that we received our bus fares to get to the theatre and nothing more. We joined to learn stagecraft, for the joy of acting and for the experience of being part of an exciting adventure. Members were recruited from the ranks of various amateur clubs in and around Glasgow, but on joining the MSU one became a professional in every possible way.

In the four years of its existence, no less than ninety-seven three-act plays were produced, fifteen of them world premieres! How was it done? On the first week of the month, we would rehearse a production. On the second week we would present the play, Monday to Saturday. On the third week, another play would be rehearsed and presented the following week and so on. How was all this achieved? The cast met at the theatre on a Sunday afternoon. The play would be cast and a full reading would take place; the first act would be moved in a rough fashion and we would go home to mug up our lines for Act I. Full rehearsal of Act I would take place on Monday night. On the Tuesday Act II would be moved and we would go home to learn our lines, to return on Wednesday for a full rehearsal of Act II. On Thursday Act III would be set and memorised for rehearsal on Friday night. Sometimes we had a Saturday as a free day. During the Sunday, from 10 am, very often until midnight, we would rehearse, rehearse, rehearse, have costume fittings and at around 7 pm, the final dress rehearsal.

The theatre only held two-hundred and fifty people but on several occasions the House Full signs were on display. Many of the plays received glowing reviews from the press and the critics made their way from London for important productions. Nevertheless, due to the fact that it was a completely independent enterprise, Molly had to consider her budget very carefully. She worked – as did her team – on all aspects of the running of the theatre. We knocked on doors all over Rutherglen selling tickets for the events. We took turns in the box office. We scrubbed floors, painted scenery and created costumes. Versatility was the watchword.

On the late afternoon of a certain opening night, Molly was by herself scrubbing out the foyer, when a group of reporters arrived and enquired of the charlady the whereabouts of Miss Urquhart.

'Haud oan therr a minute son, an ah'll see if she's in,' said Molly and she went off to the dressing room, changed her clothes and her accent and gave them their interview.

In view of all the demands placed upon the cast, and especially on Molly herself, there were times when it was impossible to be word perfect. One Friday evening, Molly was on stage with Andrew Crawford. It was freezing weather and the heating had broken down. This affected Molly and she was having difficulty remembering her lines for one particularly long speech. However, she had secreted the prompter in the fireplace. Gliding upstairs in a dramatic movement, she had a prolonged discussion with the prompter to get her lines right again.

One reviewer commented on a heavy drama: 'I thought . . . that the invalid's bed in the final act was badly placed.' The placing of the bed had been dictated by the fact that the director/manager/charlady/actress had been too hard pressed to memorise all the lines of the last act and Margaret Smith the prompter was tucked under the bed!

Molly directed every production and frequently took one of the leading roles. She was a terrific driving force and was instrumental in launching young actors into professional careers. Molly inspired many Scots actors including Gordon Jackson, Stanley Baxter, Duncan Macrae, Rona Anderson, Eileen Herlie and Nicholas Parsons.

AIRMAN

IN THE SUMMER OF 1940 as a nineteen-year old, I knew that it would not be long until I was called up to the forces, so at the beginning of June, I volunteered to join the RAF. The recruiting officer's question caught me off guard. 'Would you like to train for ground crew duties or for air crew?' As I hesitated, he mentioned that there was more money as an air crew trainee. It was suggested that I would be a suitable candidate for wireless operator/air-gunner training. I took the bait as I expected the war would be over before the end of my training. What a hope!

By 1941, RAF training camps had sprung up all over Scotland and England. Most of those camps were situated well away from civilisation, from shops, theatres, cinemas, dance halls – and girls. The initial months of service were marked by hours of square-bashing, rifle-drill and physical exercises in order to get the rookies into shape to face up to the Nazi menace.

On call-up, where was I posted to in sunny June '41? To Blackpool! To civilian digs. I had 'won a watch' indeed. Kathleen from Halifax arrived on holiday and stayed in the top floor of our billet. All residents shared the dining room and a harmonious time was had by all. Sure, we had all the tedium of countless hours of drill, but on most evenings we were free to dance at the Tower Ballroom and the Winter Gardens – all for sixpence! (2½p)

During the day, along with hundreds of other prospective wireless operators/air gunners, I was taught the intricacies of the Morse code. Burton's spacious clothing shops and warehouses were taken over as classrooms, and many trainees failed as the speed progressed from five words a minute up to thirty words a minute.

Chambers current dictionary gives the definition of 'gone for a Burton' – as airman's slang meaning dead or drowned. It has been suggested that the phrase was originally coined after an airman failed the Morse code tests at Burton's.

In the daytime I tapped away with my Morse code buzzer and in the evenings I waltzed the night away on the dance floor with Kathleen. Did I fall in love with this winsome Yorkshire lass? Of course I did. Walking home one moonlit night, we sang the popular song of the time 'Amapola' and vowed that at any time in the future when we heard 'Amapola' played, then we would think of each other. We kept in touch for a while, then she married a soldier and we wished each other well.

On completion of my wireless operator training at Blackpool, I was posted to a small transmitting station near Invergordon in the north-east of Scotland to await my gunnery course. During this time I served as a crew member on Sunderland Flying Boats. The Sunderland was developed from the Short's C Class Flying Boat that had been built in 1936 for Imperial Airways. Before the war it was used for carrying passengers and mail across the Atlantic and to the Commonwealth countries. Equipped with front and rear gun turrets, as well as port and starboard gun positions, it could carry bombs and depth charges. It was a most useful aircraft for offensive and reconnaissance missions. Twelve hour sorties and a crew of twelve made the galley retained from the civil aircraft a most welcome addition. Sunderland crews were always well fed. The Germans called the Sunderlands the 'Porcupines,' because of their all round fire power and had a great respect for them.

After Invergordon there was a posting to Yatesbury in Wiltshire for more wireless training. Then on to Pembrey in Wales for air-gunner's training and in due course I arrived in Ashbourne, Derbyshire as a fully qualified wireless operator/air gunner. At Ashbourne OTU (Operational Training Unit) I joined an air crew and trained for several months prior to being posted to Thruxton, an operational squadron in the South of England. So there I was – ready, willing and waiting to face the enemy.

Then something unusual happened which very probably saved my life. After only one week at the 'ops' squadron and without being used on any missions, our entire air-crew was returned to Ashbourne OTU. We were informed that until further notice we would be required as instructors as there was a desperate shortage of 'screens'. The posting back to Ashbourne was a mixed blessing. Most of the instructors at the unit were 'operation hardened' and experienced fliers, having done one or more tours of operation and as a reward were 'screened' from further operations for a period of time and posted to the training units to instruct the rookies.

So here I was – a 'screen' – far away from the enemy – instructing the new recruits – without ever having seen action myself. Nevertheless, I was also obliged during that time to join a crew as a wireless operator with pilots flying solo for the first time. This was hazardous in the extreme and with no chance of a medal for bravery. I flew with at least three sorry young pilots who crash-landed their aircraft and failed the course. On each occasion I managed to extricate myself from the seat and run like blazes from the crackling and smoking aircraft.

It must be realised that in the Air Force Stations in the 1940s there was no television and few radios. Consequently there was always a need for entertainment and anyone who could act, sing, dance or was generally into music, was in great demand. In the hope that I might continue in the theatre at the end of the hostilities, I took every opportunity to volunteer to act and produce at the station theatres. I gathered together singers, dancers, comedians and musicians; my concert party was complete. Sally was our Welsh soprano and sang like a lintie. She was a sergeant WAAF PTI – Physical Training Instructor – a stunning beauty with brown

33

hair, blue eyes and rosy lips. Ah, the lips! I still recall the lips. Let me explain: Sally was the only female in the PTI section. Her team members were all big strong, muscular young men mostly over six feet tall. They were a gey lusty lot and found it difficult to keep their eyes away from the attractive sergeant. Sally and I struck up a nice friendship and sat together kissing and cuddling in the station cinema. After walking her home to the WAAF quarters of an evening, I would seek out a wee bit of high ground before enjoying a goodnight embrace and kiss. She was five feet nine inches tall – I was five feet four and a half!

'You're a nice lad, Jimmy,' she explained one night, 'but you know why I allow you to take me home? I wouldn't take any chances with these big monsters in the PTI section. They're too strong for me. But I can handle you, wee Jimmy!' I did not complain. For the record – *there wis nae hanky-panky!* Sally married her tall marine boyfriend. From my sports meetings prior to joining the RAF I had collected an array of prizes including five canteens of cutlery. Sally was pleased to receive one of them as a wedding gift.

On my first arrival at Ashbourne I was promoted to the rank of sergeant. Some of the lads with outstanding exam results were promoted to the first order of Commissioned Rank – Pilot Officer. My exam results were average and, like the majority, just earned three stripes. Nevertheless, it didn't take me long to learn that a commission could be applied for at any time during RAF service. The pay for a commissioned rank was higher than that of an NCO and I knew for sure that the catering in the Officers' Mess was of a higher standard than the food in the Sergeants' Mess. Wee Jimmy boy decided to apply for a commission. I filled in the application form and waited six months for my interview.

The important day eventually arrived. My 'judge' was Squadron Leader Angus McPherson – a Scot – Hallelujah! He seemed an amiable gentleman – an experienced pilot with many flying hours to his credit and he wore the DFC and bar. 'Come in, Sergeant. Take off your hat. Sit down.' There was

silence for some time while he read over my application. 'OK, Stuart, what makes you think you deserve to be commissioned?' I didn't think it would be appropriate to admit that I was really only interested in more pay and better grub. 'Well Sir, I feel that I have genuine reasons for wanting a move from the Sergeants' mess to the Officers' mess. As an instructor I've coped well enough and I'm still waiting for a posting to an 'ops' squadron. My drama club and concert party has been successful here on the station and at the Town Hall. We've raised hundreds of pounds for our RAF benevolent fund. I want to mix with the officers and hold some auditions for new talent. Regarding sport, Sir, I'm the present Mile Champion of the squadron and I want to seek out some officers for our cross-country team. They spend too much of their free time drinking in the bar.' The Squadron Leader gave me a big smile, 'Thanks Stuart – we'll let you know.' I got my commission.

In September 1944, I was experiencing a relatively quiet war, still attached to the operational training unit in Derbyshire. I flew with pilots in training and instructed the wireless operators/air gunners. Off duty, I ran for the squadron athletics teams, produced plays and concerts and enjoyed dancing in the village. It was a good time for me. In fact, it was a great life as far as I was concerned, far away from the real action. I wasn't mad keen to be a hero. However the war was catching up on Jimmy Stuart. Field Marshall Montgomery had a daring plan. It required the American 101st and 82nd Airborne Division to capture the bridges at Eindhoven and Nijmegen respectively and for the British 1st Airborne Division to capture those around the Dutch town of Arnhem. Sadly the operation was a failure and many lives were lost. I was not involved in the operation but since many aircrews were lost, replacement crews were required. They began to arrive at Harwell RAF Station in the South of England on 28 September, 1944. Leaving from Ashbourne, I joined the crew of a Stirling aircraft piloted by Warrant Officer Dick Draper. The complete crew consisted of a pilot, navigator, bomb-aimer, flight engineer, wireless op/air gunner and a rear gunner. Dick Draper was a young Englishman from Sussex and one of the most capable captains on the station. He was also the most likeable and modest of men. Happily for me, he was to remain my skipper right until the end of my service. Our crew flew in a Stirling. The front and mid-upper turrets had been removed leaving a rear-turret only. I would have taken the place of the rear-gunner in the event of him being injured.

Ten days after I arrived at Harwell, the whole Station, including my squadron, moved to Rivenhall in Essex as part of 38 Group. This group provided aircraft (tugs) for towing large wooden and canvas gliders (models Horsa and Hamilcar) and also for carrying parachutists. Until techniques were developed to drop heavy equipment by parachute, the only method available for delivering guns, jeeps and light tanks to a battlefield overseas was by glider. Gliders could be used to transport infantry to the battlefield in concentrated groups, rather than being widely scattered in parachute 'sticks'. The squadron was equipped with converted bomber aircraft, Stirlings, Halifaxes or Albemarles. When not involved with airborne training or operations, we frequently undertook supply dropping sorties in aid of resistance forces and also occasional bombing missions. For the next six months, in all weathers, our Stirling-Horsa combinations rehearsed for what we knew would be 'The Big One' – the successful crossing of the Rhine.

At the beginning of March 1945 I was home on leave. One morning as I was making my way across Carntyne Square I was warmly greeted by two of my good friends, Mr and Mrs McVean. They were walking with the pram and signalled to me to speak quietly as the wee one had just gone to sleep. May Kelt and her soldier lad Duncan had married in March 1943 and Elizabeth arrived on the 1 February 1944. They were a very happy couple. On that same leave one of my best pals, Jimmy Spiers, invited me to be his best man at his wedding later on that month. The date was significant.

In March 1945, Adolf Hitler was not enjoying good health. His back was bent and he was a shadow of his former pomposity. He was swallowing fifty tablets a day. He had been dictator of an empire numbering three hundred million people and boasted that his empire would last a thousand years. It was crumbling after only twelve years. The Third Reich was nearing its end.

I did not show up on my pal's big day and did not communicate with him. On my return from leave we were confined to barracks. Telephone calls were not permitted and the sending of mail was suspended. We speculated. We were eager. The weather had to be right. We waited.

Came the dawn, on 24 March 1945 and the greatest airborne operation in history was about to commence. The operation code name was Varsity. Field Marshall Montgomery was informed that Prime Minister Winston Churchill wanted to watch the Allies as they crossed the last barrier on the way to Berlin. Montgomery was not at all pleased and felt that Mr Churchill would be a nuisance; however nothing could deter the old warrior. Apparently Eisenhower was not perturbed and told one of his commanders to make sure there was a good supply of Scotch whisky for 'Winnie'.

Churchill sent this message to the troops: 'British soldiers – it will long be told how, with our Canadian brothers and valiant United States Allies, this superb task was accomplished. Once the river line is pierced and the crust of German resistance is broken, decisive victory in Europe will be near. May God prosper our arms in the noble adventure after our long struggle for King and Country, for dear life and for the freedom of mankind.'

What a morning! Thousands of allied paratroops and airborne troops, packed into a gigantic airborne assault, swarmed across the Rhine ready to swamp the enemy. For the first time airborne troops flew simultaneously into battle from British and Continental bases, pouring across the already breached Rhine in a double stream that seemed endless – 1,500 air transports carrying 40,000 sky-men.

From airfields all over Britain and the Continent, streams of tow-planes, gliders and troop carriers poured for hours after dawn. Captain Dick Draper shook hands with our glider pilot and with each one of his crew. My logbook tells me that we were airborne at 7.10 am. I soon watched, above and below me a bewildering conglomeration of planes, all heading for the Rhine. Long before we reached the English coast huge American bombers were passing high overhead on bombing missions in support of the ground and airborne attack. Nearing the landing zones the great American stream on our right surged along parallel with us and, bunch by bunch, the fighter cover began to whirl overhead and below.

As we edged towards the Rhine the first Dakotas streaked away below us on the way home. The Rhine, shrouded in smoke for miles, appeared as a silver strand across the fields and in a few seconds there came a dramatic call from our navigator – 'We're over the river, lads!' The next murderous ten minutes I shall never forget. The air seethed with planes in every direction. Behind us our Horsa glider, crammed full of resolute soldiers, went into 'high tow' in readiness for the release. We held unswervingly to the course. There was a last exchange of words on the intercom between our pilot and the glider pilot: 'Good Luck.' 'Thanks for the tow – see you soon.' The towrope was cast off and down went our glider through the flak and away in a steep turn. In our few hectic minutes over the target area it was possible to look down on a mass of parachutes which made the air look as if a giant thistledown had been destroyed by a gale.

We turned to port when we had released our glider. The sky was criss-crossed with tracer bullets and exploding shells. Dick pushed the control column forward and our huge Stirling dived. 'That's it boys – let's go home for lunch.'

I was later to learn that, as we flew home safely to our base, my soldier friend Duncan McVean had been killed on the ground below me. So for me, on this historic day, certainly the most momentous of my life, I was not aware that my future wife back home in Glasgow had just become a widow. May was hanging out the baby's washing in the back garden when the telegram was handed to her. Duncan would not be coming home. She was twenty-three – Elizabeth was thirteen months. The war with Germany was to end a few weeks later.

The conflict was nearing its end and yet on 7 April, in a freak act of warfare almost overlooked by historians, German ME-109 fighters undertook a massive suicide mission against American bomber formations over Hanover. Having despaired of challenging the allied armadas by conventional tactics, the Luftwaffe recruited one hundred and eighty four volunteer pilots to ram the Flying Fortresses in mid-air. In that day's action, one hundred and thirty-three German ME-109s were lost, with the lives of seventy-seven pilots, for the destruction of twenty-three bombers. At this, its last gasp, the Nazi empire could still summon extraordinary reserves of fanaticism to mark its death throes.

On VE Day, 8 May, 1945 I was on leave with my navigator pal, Howard Brown. We mingled with the jubilant crowds in Trafalgar Square and stood in front of Buckingham Palace waving, along with thousands of thankful people, to the King and Queen and the two princesses and of course Winston Churchill, on the balcony.

On 13 June our crew made the first of several supply-dropping flights in Stirling Aircraft to Norway with much needed medical supplies. After unloading at the airfield, on this first day, we had some time to spare and were driven by Jeep into Oslo. As we drove the fifteen miles from the airport to the city, the villagers and especially the children seemed to be aware of our arrival in their beloved land and were excitedly waving small Norwegian flags and cheering us like conquering heroes.

The city centre seemed extremely busy and we soon learned the reason for the crowds. King Haakon was due to return to the Royal Palace after five years of forced exile in London. Lined up outside the palace on a downward slope were about two thousand singers – choirs gathered from all around Norway ready to sing a welcome to their Monarch.

Arriving at the back of the mass of people, my rear-gunner and I could barely see the palace balcony, so we climbed a tree to get a better view. Two palace guards, noting we were RAF airmen, waved us down from our perch. We gave them some bars of chocolate, which of course they had not seen for years, whereupon they escorted us up to the front of the action. The King appeared and we listened to beautiful singing from the many assembled choirs.

After the celebrations at the palace we made our way to the Public Square. The place was packed with joyful people. Both men and women had donned their national dress and the colours were magnificent. Flags, banners and garlands were hung from every vantage point and several bands played at the same time. Beer and champagne was in short supply. No matter. Norway was drunk with happiness. The dancing was hilarious. Paddy and I were hysterical with laughter when we managed to persuade two bonny blonde maids to waltz with us on the cobblestones. They had little English but we managed to communicate. We missed the jeep arranged to take us back to the airport but managed to hitch a lift after an incredible night.

After VE Day our crews were engaged in flights to Germany to bring home prisoners of war to the UK. I would like to report that those were joyous experiences and, of course, to a great extent they were. However, my memories of those flights are rather sombre. Our Stirling was packed each time with as many men as we could cram into it. The POWs were mostly quiet and withdrawn. We were caring towards them but it wasn't our place to quiz them about their time in captivity. Many of them were pale and emaciated. They all stank to high heaven and – pour souls – had to submit to delousing immediately on landing. My abiding memory of those times was when we approached the white cliffs of Dover. Everybody – but everybody – shed tears.

In October 1945 our crew was posted to RAF Station Cairo West, where we were based until we were 'demobbed' in April

1946. We flew from our station in the South of England on a cold, miserable, rainy day and eight hours later landed in North Africa. We stopped overnight and the next day, after five hours, arrived in Cairo West in the Egyptian heat of 90°F. This was going to be a pleasant way to end my service.

During the winter our crew flew on missions to North Africa, Malta and Italy. I had the opportunity of attending the famous San Carlo Opera House in Naples and heard the great Italian baritone Tito Gobbi. The opera was *La Traviata*. In my time I've witnessed a few standing ovations but never one to match that occasion in Naples. The sight and sound of three thousand excited Italians standing, clapping, smiling and shouting 'Bravo! Bravo!' was a spectacle to behold and remember.

I recall another off-duty day when I was stationed at Cairo West. The great pyramids of Giza had to be visited and, along with my pilot, Dick and Paddy our rear-gunner, I stood in awe beside the great tombs. The three pyramids of Giza are the greatest of the many pyramids in Egypt and the most famous. The largest pyramid – Khufu (2,600BC) is 768 feet square and 482 feet high. It covers thirteen acres, took twenty years to build and is constructed of 2,3000,000 huge blocks of limestone, fitted together with great accuracy. I knew I might never get another chance: 'Well, lads – how about it? Who's for Khufu?' Dick laughed. 'Jock you're mad! You'll break your legs. Forget it!' The thought of climbing the world's highest pyramid was too great a temptation and off I jogged to the base of the edifice. It was a fantastic and exciting experience to 'pech' and sclim up and over the huge blocks. I was surprised to see that each one was about three feet in height so it was a slow climb. However, in the previous week I had won the RAF (Egypt) Mile Championship, so I knew I was in peak fitness. 'Mad Jock' reached the summit and waved to his companions far below. On reflection, it was a bit foolhardy. I didn't realise how dangerous it was and I understand that because of so many accidents, the climbing of the Great Pyramids is no longer permitted.

One cherished memory of my time in Egypt was on a return flight from the UK. We had been on a week's leave and were just about to land at our base at Cairo West. The date was 13 April 1946 and 139,468 football fans were packed into Glasgow's Hampden Stadium for the Victory International; Scotland versus England. I had been following the match on the radio and as the only Scot on board had been taking some barracking from the English supporters in the crew. As we landed and taxied along the runway my earphones seemed to explode with the sound of the famous Hampden Roar. With the score at 0–0 and only sixty seconds to go, Jackie Husband of Partick Thistle took a free kick. It was headed on by my Rangers hero, Deedle Dawdell, Willie Waddell. Celtic's Jimmy Delaney was in the goalmouth and rammed the ball into the English net for a glorious victory! What a GAME! What a happy day!

On Saturday 4 May 1946 I joyfully embarked on a troop ship at Port Said and, in glorious sunny weather, sailed through the Mediterranean and disembarked at Toulon in the south of France at 11 pm on Friday 10 May. Then came a long train journey viewing the liberated French countryside and stopping at Calais on the Sunday at 10 am. A welcome meal followed before boarding ship again for the last lap and arrival on British soil.

The big hall at London's Olympia was a hive of activity. I received a gratuity of £75 and made my way to the civilian clothing store. Scenes of hysterical laughter ensued as suits, sports jackets, raincoats and hats of varying styles were tried on. After five years of nothing but a service uniform it was a pantomime to see my mates in pork pie hats and pin-stripe suits!

On Tuesday 14 May at 11.30 am I was officially released from the Royal Air Force and at nine o'clock I arrived in my home city of Glasgow and into my mother's loving arms.

Food rationing was still in force. It was great to be home, but I knew that I would miss the fresh fruit that I had become used to – pears, oranges, dates and bananas. Some young children had never tasted these delights. The government even held a banana day when every child under eighteen years of age was presented with one banana!

The kit bag was opened and all the Egyptian treasures were revealed – Cairo watches, exotic fans, models of the Pyramids and the Sphinx and two dozen bananas!

BERTHA WADDELL

DURING MY RAF SERVICE I approached Mr Matthew Forsyth, producer of the Glasgow Citizen's Theatre Company, with a view to employment when I was released. He gave me a warm welcome when I was demobbed in May 1946 and we chatted in his office about my Air Force career. He reckoned that he would be happy to have me in his company, but not right away.

However he had an idea which would enable me to gain more first class professional experience. I was to contact Miss Bertha Waddell in Blantyre and explain that he had recommended me. The following day I found myself in a large house in Blantyre, ten miles from Glasgow, being interviewed for an acting job by two charming middle-aged spinster sisters, Bertha and Jenny Waddell. Bertha asked me if I could sing. I told her I didn't consider myself much of a vocalist. Even so, she made me sing and seemed to think that I would pass muster. She asked me to dance an old-time waltz with her and then perform somersaults in her hallway! Next I was asked to make some funny faces like a pantomime clown. That wis nae bother to me: playing the fool was one of my hobbies. Acting and miming tests followed and after about an hour it was time to relax and have a coffee. I then signed a one-year contract with the Bertha Waddell Children's Theatre Company. It was a fully professional company and actor's equity rates were honoured.

Bertha Waddell was the daughter of a Glasgow architect. As a child she showed singing talent and Sir Hugh Roberton of Glasgow Orpheus Choir fame suggested that she should

45

compete in the Glasgow Music Festival. She won first prize at the age of eleven. In 1928, aged twenty, she had the idea of starting a children's theatre presenting plays, fairy stories, music, mime and dancing. Sponsored by the Scottish Committee of the Arts Council, Bertha and her sister had their base at Caldergrove House near Blantyre, Lanarkshire. For ten months of the year they toured, mainly schools, and during the summer break, designed and made costumes and painted props. Bertha wrote plays and dramatised rhymes and songs. Jenny arranged traditional folk airs and played the piano for the group. There were two repertoires. One for the 5–9 year-old group, the other for 9–12 year-olds. All the company members (six in total, three men and three women) were professional adult actors, singers and dancers. Everything was packed into a small van with one member at the wheel and another as passenger. A car followed with the other players. We toured all over Britain – Glasgow, Edinburgh, Manchester, London and Newcastle. My one season with the company seemed to pass very quickly but I must say it was a great joy to be involved entertaining the wee ones.

At the start of each performance, Jenny would pop her head through the curtains and sing 'Cuckoo! Cuckoo!' Then she would announce 'Item Number One – The Greedy Boy,'or Ten Green Bottles or whatever, then again 'Item Number One!' The children joined in at every opportunity and screamed with glee at the comedy routines. I danced, I sang, I mimed. I acted the young lord, the old Russian gypsy and the clown in the pantomime. My singing improved during the tour.

The company was wound up in its fortieth anniversary year in 1968. Bertha Waddell's Theatre Company was honoured with giving six command performances at Glamis, Balmoral and one at Buckingham Palace. The first occasion was in 1933 for the Princesses Elizabeth and Margaret.

GINGER'S MILE

❦❦❦

AS A BOY MY MAIN INTEREST was football. I loved the game but I'm afraid I was a dead loss in the soccer arena. I was never picked for any of the teams at primary or secondary school. Even at the Boys' Brigade five-a-side games I was usually the last to be selected.

My interest in running started in 1933 when the CAAC (Carntyne Amateur Athletics Club) was formed. There seemed to be hundreds of young people living in the Carntyne housing scheme at that time and the formation of an athletic club took off in a big way. During the winter months we went for cross-country runs (usually three or four miles) on Tuesday and Thursday evenings. Races or inter-club events took place on Saturday afternoons. We were all novices at running, but even at thirteen years of age I was capable of keeping up with the older members of the club.

In the early summer of 1934 I entered for the Boys' Brigade local district Athletics Championships and, wearing my CAAC vest and new spiked track running shoes, I reported to the stadium ready to do battle. I was last in my heat of the 100 yards, last in my heat of the 220 yards, knocked the bar down at my first attempt at the high jump and at throwing the cricket ball, I failed to get past the first round. I was a broken wee lad! I shed my expensive track spikes and put on my sannies. Sergeant Young saw my distress: 'I was just thinking, Ginger, you would probably be more suited to the half-mile race. It's the last event tonight. You ran well in the cross-country training. You've got good stamina.' I appreciated his interest but explained to him that the half-mile was open only to boys of sixteen or over. 'You leave that to me, Ginger! I'll speak to the officer-in-charge. I'm sure I can swing it for you.'

Big Walter was as good as his word. There was an entry of about twenty lads for the race, but most of them were untrained or had started smoking and lacked the necessary puff to stay the distance. Still in my sannies I was the happy winner of the race and realised from then on that I was destined to be a middle-distance performer.

I went on to win the Glasgow Battalion BB Mile Championship and led the CAAC in winning the Scottish Youths' cross-country Championship at our first attempt. At the Rangers FC Sports Meeting at Ibrox Park in 1938, I was invited to line up, with others, in an attempt on the 1500 metres world record. Sydney Wooderson, the London athlete and holder of the world mile record, was the star athlete that day. I served as pace-maker and Wooderson clocked 3 minutes, 49 seconds – just one second off the record.

When I was in the RAF I won the Cairo Mile Trophy and in 1946 won the Scottish five-mile cross-country novice championship from a field of two hundred and eighty competitors at Pollok Park.

Sadly, after the war the C.A.A.C. did not re-form, so I joined Shettleston Harriers. One event, which sticks in my mind, was a one-mile handicap race at Helenvale Park, Glasgow. I was in good form at the time and started as the 'scratch man' on ten yards giving allowances (ie starts) up to one hundred and sixty yards, over the four quarter-mile laps. Forty competitors lined up. It is always entertaining for spectators to see the scratch man slowly but surely going through the pack, and more particularly if he is successful. On this occasion I ploughed my way through the entire field.

The following morning the *Daily Record* carried a bold headline:

STUART WINS BRILLIANT MILE. The reporter then went on to describe the race: 'Diminutive Ginger Stuart of Shettleston Harriers was in great form last night . . .' My mother enquired of me 'James, what exactly does he mean by "diminutive"?' I replied, 'Mother, he means very, very small.' 'Cheek of him, son!' my mother huffed. 'Imagine calling you small.'

Ah well! A mother's love!

◉ ◉ ◉

THE CITZ

◉ ◉ ◉

MATTHEW FORSYTH WAS AS GOOD as his word. At the start of the 1947–48 season at the Citizens' Theatre I was signed on contract with another young actor by the name of Andrew Buggy. Andrew later changed his name to Andrew Keir. We were both signed up for two years as members of the company and were expected to double as ASMs (Assistant Stage Managers.)

I had the satisfaction of working at the 'Citz' until 1957 (latterly as a freelance member) and acted alongside some players who became very successful in television, pantomime and films. Molly Urquhart, Stanley Baxter, Roddy McMillan, Fulton MacKay, John Fraser, Madeline Christie and John Cairney all appeared at the Citizens' Theatre.

My most abiding memory at the Citz was knowing and working with the great Scottish actor, Duncan Macrae.

In 1943 John Duncan Macrae left teaching to go full-time as a professional actor, at the same time dropping his first name to become known as Duncan Macrae. He trod the boards in Scotland and in London's West End for almost twenty-five years and is arguably the greatest actor Scotland has ever produced. Macrae excelled in all types of productions. He was a first-class dramatic actor, brilliant in comedy roles and was also very successful as a pantomime dame. His films include *Whisky Galore, The Kidnappers, Tunes of Glory* and *Casino Royale*. He was cast as skipper Para Handy on television in the first series of *The Vital Spark*.

Off stage, he was a gentle, caring, intellectual man. In appearance he was tall, about six feet in height, very lean and muscular. Some critics referred to him as Big Skinnymalinky.

Amazingly enough, John Duncan Macrae's main claim to fame in the eyes of some people was that he sang a daft wee song called 'The Wee Cock Sparra' on BBC Television on Hogmany 1959.

I remember doing a double act with Macrae in a variety bill at the theatre in Kilmarnock. The sketch was titled 'The Mighty Mauler.' Macrae was a champion wrestler matched with an imaginary opponent. I was his trainer and the commentator at the event. Here's the gist of it:

The trainer enters dressed in a white track suit and sporting a tartan bunnet.

TRAINER: Ladies and gentlemen, it is my proud privilege tonight to introduce to you the most superb specimen of magnificent manhood that the Scottish Nation has ever produced! He is a wrestler beyond compare – a man of steel and whipcord – a terror to his opponents. Ladies and gentlemen – let's hear it for – Mauler Macrae!

Mauler enters, bows and smiles inanely. He proceeds to go through his pre-fight bending and stretching routine.

TRAINER: Now folks, Mauler is about to unveil to you the body that is a monument to physical fitness. Wonder Boy – let the public see the torso of the century!

The dressing gown is discarded to loud cheers! The body is revealed – bare chest, yellow long johns. With incredible contortions Mauler continues to limber up.

TRAINER: 'Now folks, you are about to witness the pride of Polmadie, Mauler Macrae in action, in a grand exhibition bout with the champion of the Gallowgate – Twister McTurk.

The trainer turns round and notes that Mauler is lying flat on his back in some discomfort.

TRAINER: Up now, Mauler – here we go!

MAULER: Ah cannae!

TRAINER: Whit dae ye mean – ye cannae?

MAULER: Ah shoudny hiv ett thae three fish suppers oan tap o ma tea. Ah think ah've goat cramp in ma kyte!

After a struggle, the trainer gets Mauler to his feet. There's a sound of loud creaking.

TRAINER: Aye, aye, Mauler – a wee bit creaky?

MAULER: That's funny – ah wis well oiled last night.

The fight commences and lasts several minutes. The bell rings. Mauler flops into his chair, lies back and groans.

MAULER: Aw jings! Ah'm jiggert!

TRAINER: Away ye go man. He huznae touched ye yet!

MAULER: Huznae touched me? Well, there's somebody in here that's goat a helluva spite at me!

Suddenly Mauler produces a huge wooden mallet from under the mat and knocks out his opponent.

TRAINER: Twister McTurk is out! Mauler Macrae wins with his famous hammer blow. Ladies and gentlemen another glorious triumph for Scotland's mightiest wrestler!

Mauler raises his arms, then falls flat on his face unconscious!

I suppose every athlete dreams of being a champion. I decided to make a bid for one of the track titles at the Scottish Amateur Athletics Championships to be held at Hampden Park on a Saturday in June 1948. I'd had a successful cross-country season with the Shettleston Harriers and at the start of the track season, had won several mile races; I knew I would be at the peak of my fitness at the beginning of June.

My favourite race was the mile and I had competed many times over the distance both in scratch and handicap races. However the quality of mile runners at that time was very high and I was pretty sure that I would be pushed even to win a medal. I'd had a little experience over the three miles and the six miles, but not enough to give me confidence at Championship level.

'How about the two mile steeplechase?' I thought. I had never competed in a steeplechase event. It's a race that needs middle distance pace coupled with a big helping of stamina. My mile racing speed would serve me well and I had proved my stamina over cross-country races up to ten miles long.

My Parents' Wedding Day, Glasgow 1913

Top: 'The Three Apostles' – left to right; Peter, James and John

Middle: Left to right; John, James, Ronald and Peter with Mum and Dad (1948)

Bottom: Left to right; John, James, Ronald and Peter (Kelso 1995)

With wavy hair (1945)

My pilot Dick Draper – Cairo West, RAF
Station (December 1945)

With my daughter Fiona we had a joyous reunion with Dick (1995)

Top: The clown in *Harlequinade,* Bertha Waddell Children's Theatre (1946)

Left: Rab and Teenie (Margaret Christie) Graham Moffat's *Bunty Pulls the Strings* (1949)

Bottom: Stanley Baxter (centre), JS as the wee sailor, at my elbow Joan Sims, of 'Carry On' Film fame, Citizen's Theatre Pantomime *The Happy Hap'ny* (1951)

Top left: Winning the Scottish Two
Miles Steeplechase from JC Ross,
Shettleston Harriers (Hampden, 1948)

Top right: Swanage Summer Show (1952)

Bottom: Addressing our National Dish (1997)

An engaging evening with May (1953)

Elizabeth and Iain – their big day
(1968)

Fiona and Martin – their big day (1995)

Top left: My dear wife, May (1980)

Top right: Elizabeth and my first granddaughter Kirsty (1976)

Bottom left: My daughters Fiona and Elizabeth with granddaughter Kirsty (1987)

Bottom right: Elizabeth and Kirsty (Glasgow University 1998)

Top left: 'Conqueror of Masada' (1983)

Top right: Papa and his two Princesses, Shona and Gillian (Sarawak 1999)

Bottom: In the presence of HRH Princess Anne, preparing to say grace at a *Save the Children Charity* Lunch (1995)

The steeplechase is a gruelling event – eight quarter-mile laps, each containing four three-foot hurdles and one hurdle complete with a water jump. I checked on the possible contenders for this title and reckoned I might have a reasonable chance.

There was however one big hurdle to overcome before I lined up on the track. I was of course under contract to the Citz and matinees took place on Saturday afternoons. Then I discovered that the format for Championship programmes was for the steeplechase to be the final event of the afternoon.

The scheduled play at the Citz was Chekhov's *The Cherry Orchard*. I had a part in the play but did not appear in the third act. Yes! It might just be possible to keep myself really busy on that particular Saturday afternoon. The producer gave me permission to be absent from the final curtain call at the end of the play. All that was required now was to arrange for a fast taxi to take me from the stage-door in the Gorbals to the stadium at Hampden.

The day arrives. The play begins. I play my part in the first and second acts. I sprint out of the stage door and into the waiting taxi. My minder, brother Ron, is there with a flask of coffee. I shed my stage costume and make-up and don my running gear. The weather is fine and there are no traffic hold-ups. Hampden hoves into view. I check my watch. We might just make it. Ron pays the taxi driver and I jog into the Competitors' Reporting Room and receive my race number for my vest.

'Attention please! Will all competitors for the steeplechase report to the starting line.'

I had made it !

In the taxi I had been massaging my legs with olive oil and now had a few seconds to jog up and down to warm up before arriving as the last athlete on the line.

The starter's gun triggered a dozen runners into action. Ron joined my older brother Peter in the stand and even on my first lap I could hear them shouting for me. At the bell with one lap remaining, I was running neck and neck with Jim C Ross, a fellow member of Shettleston Harriers. He was older than me, one of Scotland's most graceful runners and a former steeplechase champion. We were still together on the bend after the bell. Up the back straight we were locked together and stride for stride we remained so round the final bend and into the home straight. Ron and Peter were losing their voices. The tape came into view and Wee Jimmy Stuart was the victor by about ten yards.

After the medal ceremony and official photographs, it was back to the 'smell of the greasepaint and the roar of the crowd!'

When the Edinburgh Festival Committee announced early in 1948 that the major drama production that year was to be the great Scottish morality play – *The Three Estates* – to say that most people were sceptical would be an understatement. Nevertheless, there were some who felt it was appropriate to produce the archaic Scottish Masterpiece at a Scottish-based festival, however limited the appeal.

The Three Estates by Sir David Lindsay was first performed at Linlithgow in January 1540, before the King and Queen. The second production was at Cupár, Fife, in 1552. Another presentation was given at Calton Hill, Edinburgh in 1554. At the time the play was written, Lindsay was about fifty-four. He had studied at St Andrews and afterwards entered the Royal household, as Lord Lyon, King at Arms and an Envoy. The play so enraged the Scottish clergy of the time that they ordered the manuscript to be burned by the public executioner in 1558, three years after the author's death.

In the autumn of 1948 the entire company of the Citizens' Theatre was involved in a memorable enterprise. Playwright James Bridie, producer Tyrone Guthrie and Festival Director Rudolph Bing planned the project. It was a joint theatrical presentation between the Citizens' Theatre, Unity, Dundee and Perth Repertory Companies. The playwright Robert Kemp was commissioned to adapt the text and Tyrone Guthrie (later to be knighted) directed the play.

The first objective was to find a hall large enough to encompass the complex staging requirements. Eventually it was suggested that the Church of Scotland Assembly Hall at the top of the Mound might be worth examination. Tyrone Guthrie knew he was home as soon as the gaunt silhouette of the twin-towered hall loomed into view in the shadow of the historic castle, high above and far removed from the bustle of Princes Street.

I was cast in one of the principal roles, Sandy Solace the inebriated courtier. Solace, a rumbustious loud-mouthed character, suited me fine. During a dance scene in the court, Guthrie wanted some lively action so he asked me to perform cartwheels in time to the music.

In all, there were thirty-two speaking parts. Forty-eight extras played the members of the estates, townsfolk and soldiers. In addition there were singers and musicians, making it a vast undertaking. The following brief summary of the play was given in the programme:

Diligence, a herald, summons *The Three Estates* of the realm, namely *Spiritualitie,* or Church, *Temporalitie* or Lords and the *Burgesses* or merchants. The poor people of the realm also appear unbidden. *Diligence* makes a little speech to the audience beseeching their silence and craving their patience.

The King of Humanity appears with his courtiers *Wantonness, Placebo* and *Solace.* These young men encourage the King to send for *Dame Sensualitie.* They argue and laugh him out of his scruples in the matter of lechery and the court surrenders to the charms of *Sensualitie* and her handmaidens.

Good Counsel arrives, laments the bad company and bad ways into which *King Humanitie* has fallen and resolves to seek opportunity to influence the King.

Now appear the three vices – *Flatterie, Falsehood* and *Deceit* – presented in the manner of the Medieval Theatre as three clowns. They disguise themselves, present themselves to the king and flatter themselves into positions of importance in the realm.

Under the influence of *Sensualitie* and the three vices, the King denies access to *Good Counsel* and causes *Dames Veritie* and *Chastitie* to be cast into the stocks.

At this point, just before the realm is totally ruined and utterly possessed by wickedness, comes *Divine Correction.* The vices flee the land stealing the King's treasure. Virtue is restored. *Sensualitie,* chased from the King is received by *Spiritualitie* and the King, surrounded now by *Veritie, Chastitie* and *Good Counsel* makes promise of amendment and is ordered by *Divine Correction* to summon *The Three Estates* to Parliament to make reforms.

In the first part of the play Sir David Lindsay is concerned with the moral illness and cure of the individual personified by *King Humanitie*. The second part deals with sickness and restoration of the body politic.

It opens with a farcical interlude between *Poor Man* in search of justice and a fraudulent friar selling pardons and bogus relics. This interlude establishes the two main themes of the second part of the work; namely the oppression of the poor and the corruption of the Church.

Poor Man and *Pardoner* fight and are chased off the scene by *Diligence* to make room for *The Three Estates* who enter backwards as an outward and visible sign of political retrogression.

When *The Three Estates* are seated *Divine Correction* bids *Diligence* show that it is their will that every man oppressed makes his complaint. *John the Commonweal* – symbolic figure of the embattled worker and champion of the far weaker, sillier *Poor Man*, makes forcible accusation that *The Three Estates* are led by *Flatterie, Falsehood* and *Deceit*. These three are soon flung into the stocks and *John* goes on to make more detailed complaints against the abuses of power by *Spirtualitie*. The needed reforms are agreed by the other two estates in view of their two to one majority in the house. *John the Commonweal* is presented with a bright cloak – symbolic of a *Labour Peerage*, while the leaders of *Spiritualitie,* politically, intellectually, morally and financially smashed are submitted to physical humiliation.

Proceedings are brought to a cheerful close by the public execution of *Falsehood* and *Deceit*. *Flatterie*, the meanest of the three vices is allowed to escape having taken advantage of a moment of indulgence, indeed of negligence, on the part of *Divine Correction*. The escape and apparent negligence are no less allegorical than the rest of the play and are particularly typical of Lindsay's method of conveying his more significant observations by humorous implications rather than explicit and didactic statement.

57

On Tuesday 24 August 1948, under Guthrie's inspired direction, the long dormant play sprang to renewed life on the specially constructed apron stage in the Assembly Hall. No one could have predicted its phenomenal success. The press unstintingly acknowledged the credit due to Guthrie, but accorded almost equal weight to the brilliance of the performances. The Scotsman declared: 'The whole cast was obviously in love with what it is doing, and there is such uniform excellence of playing that it seems almost ungrateful to mention individual actors. But Duncan Macrae's wonderful clowning in the dual role of *Flatterie* and the *Pardoner* was a masterpiece of a flavour as Scottish as whisky. But the real triumph was in the wonderful direction. It is nothing less than a landmark in the history of the European Theatre.'

The production became the smash-hit of the Festival. There were long queues at the box office every day and Full House signs were displayed at matinees. There was a resurgence of pride in the Scottish theatre.

James Bridie was justifiably proud of his Glasgow Citizens' people, who had not only played the leading roles but had also supplied both management and production teams. Characteristically impish he indulged in a little exaggeration in a lecture to the Royal Philosophical Society of Glasgow, claiming that the play was now the talk of the civilised world.

I have one lovely memory of *The Three Estates*: during the early rehearsals Macrae was in his element, clearly enjoying his roles and feeling very much in tune with the producer, Tyrone Guthrie. However during the second week of rehearsals he had to contend with an unexpected slap in the face. In one scene he was delivering a long speech on centre stage. In the background at the bottom of some stairs a group of townspeople were called upon to shout out with loud protests. One young member of the crowd went over the top and began gesticulating and screaming in an alarming fashion. This upset Macrae and just as he was about to appeal to Guthrie to put an end to the overacting of the young man, Guthrie halted the action. Addressing the crowd at the bottom of the stairs he stretched himself to his full height of six foot three and pointed to the loud-mouthed walk-on:

'You boy! Yes! You! Stand up!'

A tall handsome youth with long black hair raised himself from the steps. Guthrie smiled at the lad and instructed him in his impeccable Oxford accent, 'I like what you're doing dear boy, don't change a thing. By the way, what's your name?'

The answer came in a firm clear voice. 'John Cairney, sir.'

Macrae shook his head.

In due course, Guthrie took a keen interest in John Cairney's career. John went on to become successful on stage, radio, television and films. He was an outstanding Hamlet at the Citz and for ten years toured internationally presenting his own dramatised version of the life of Scotland's Bard, Robert Burns. He emigrated to New Zealand with his wife Alannah a few years ago.

I've read about stage understudies taking over from the star of the show, performing very well and thereafter going on to fame and fortune. I remember two occasions when I took over from established actors at the Citizens' Theatre at the last moment (and not even as the understudy). Alas it did not increase my fame – or fortune.

The Forrigan Reel by James Bridie was one of the plays in the Citz repertoire in which Duncan Macrae excelled. During the run of the play the company was rehearsing for 'The Scottish Play' – *Macbeth*. I think it would be true to say that some performers in the theatre are superstitious types. Some can also tell tall tales. Be that as it may, the production of *Macbeth* on stage seems to have brought about many upsets. Our Glasgow production was not spared.

In September 1949, on the last Friday of *The Forrigan Reel*'s run Macrae broke his ankle. He was taken to hospital and after examination it was decided that he was in no condition to perform on the Saturday afternoon and evening.

The producer John Casson (son of Dame Sybil Thorndyke) called a crisis meeting for the Saturday morning at 8.30 am. Various different suggestions were bandied about as to how the star's role could be filled. Jimmy Gibson, playing a smaller part, was willing to read the Macrae part and an assistant manager could read Jimmy Gibson's part. John Casson considered himself for the main part.

I was cast in a non-speaking role and appeared only in the third act. I also shared duties as prompter in the production. We had performed *The Forrigan Reel* once before and I had been fascinated by Macrae's acting. So much so, that being 'on the book' as prompter for weeks on end I was very familiar with the script and had (as an exercise for my own benefit) memorised most of the big speeches. Lennox Milne, Gudrun Ure, Laurence Hardy and Lea Ashton all made various suggestions, but John Casson kept swithering.

It was only my second season with the company and I was still learning the ropes. Even so I sensed the opportunity. 'Just an idea, Mr Casson,' I volunteered, 'I have most of John's speeches memorised.' Duncan Macrae was always referred to by his first name by members of the company. 'I could manage the part without a script, having been the prompter all these weeks.' There was silence for a wee while. Jimmy Gibson more or less took the decision for John Casson. 'Good idea, James! We'll need to cut a bit off the costume.' Macrae was eight inches taller than me. From 9 am until the curtain up at 2.30 pm. I rehearsed non-stop with Jimmy Gibson. During that matinee I only used the script once to read a vital speech and all went fine in the evening show.

As far as I was concerned, the main drama occurred at the beginning of the third act during the afternoon. In the play, Macrae, as the bizarre Highland dancer, injures his leg and has to hobble on a single crutch. We had altered the costume for me without any problems, but had not rehearsed with the crutch. I was almost due to go on stage when the props person handed me the crutch. I was dangling in mid-air! We screamed for Jimmy McCreadie the stage carpenter to bring his saw. With only seconds to go, he lopped eight inches off the crutch and I stomped into action. A Sunday newspaper had the headline: 'Steeplechaser Takes The Lead at The Citizens' !'

Roddy McMillan and Fulton Mackay were well-loved members of the Citz and both became famous on television – Roddy as Para Handy in *The Vital Spark* and Fulton as the stony-faced warder in *Porridge*. In one of the Christmas pantos they played The Broker's Men, joking, singing and dancing throughout the show. For whatever reason I can't remember, one Saturday matinee, Fulton did not arrive at the theatre. Once again the producer called me from the prompt corner and decided that I should partner Roddy.

Using a script would have been a clumsy handicap, so with Roddy's help we gagged our way through the afternoon. I was pleased to see Fulton arrive at teatime.

LOBEY DOSSER

Bud Neil was arguably Scotland's greatest strip cartoonist. He began his successful newspaper career in 1944 and five years later he created Lobey Dosser, the Sheriff of Calton Creek, considered by many to be the zenith of his creative output. The strip was an immediate success and acquired something of a cult following. Lobey Dosser celebrated his fiftieth birthday in 1999. The comic creation first appeared in the *Glasgow Evening Times* in 1949 but, nearly thirty years after his creator's death, Lobey's still a best seller.

In 1950, the pantomine at the Citz was *Red Riding Hood* and one of the highlights was a Lobey Dosser sketch. Andrew Keir, the Shotts miner who went on to become an internationally successful film actor played Rank Bajin and I was cast as Lobey Dosser. Here it is!

Shots, shouts and the sound of general turmoil off-stage. Enter Sheriff LOBEY DOSSER, *replacing a gun in his holster. He sits down at a desk.*

LOBEY: Jings! Awfy busy this weather; busier than a pup wi' fleas! Aw weel – whit hiv we got the day? (*He picks up papers from his desk.*) Wanted for murder . . . wan ear Kelly . . . carries knives, bombs and an arsenal o' assorted firearms . . . this man is a killer . . . five hunner dollars reward, deid or alive. Hmm right,then ah doot we'll no be lookin afy hard for wan ear Kelly! (*A knock is heard*) Come in! (*Enter* RANK BAJIN, *a gun in each hand.*) Aw! It's jist you! Ya chancer!

RANK: Kindly terminate the badinage, Dosser. Were it good badinage I would not complain, but your badinage happens to be rank. In other words, it is Rank Badinage, ho, ho, ho!

LOBEY: Aboot as funny as a sair heid! Whose bandage are ye talkin aboot anyway, if it's no too cheeky?

RANK: The word Dosser, is badinage, ignorant wee man!

LOBEY: Aw, don't gie us nane o the auld flannel; ye'll hiv me blushin. Ah jist hope ye're no usin sweery words in ma office.

RANK: For your elucidation, my friend: according to my Oxford dictionary badinage is light raillery.

LOBEY: Oh aye – like the wan that rins oot tae Porcupine Gulch?

RANK: Let us cease this peroration. I have come Dosser to ask for the loan of ten dollars until next week. Last evening I had the great misfortune to be robbed of my wallet in the low dive where I partake of the odd noggin.

LOBEY: Somebody robbed ye? Tut, tut, tut . . . ye should hiv come an tell't me. Ah'm the Sheriff here ye ken.

RANK: I would indeed have hastened. However enough of that! The impoverished tenants of the noisy hovels, of which I am the factor, are also behind in their payments. Why, only this afternoon I had occasion to evict an old lady of ninety-eight, lock and stock.

LOBEY: Whit happened tae her barrel?

RANK: Out with them! Into the snow I say! Little mercy can they expect from Rank Bajin – villain!

LOBEY: D'ye ken this, Bajin – yir a nae-yooser. You'd flog yer Grannie's top set for a tanner . . . you'd flog a deid horse. Ther's somethin up with ye. Ye could nae huv got yer cod liver ile an orange juice when you were wee . . . yir a pest . . . yir . . .

RANK: Careful Dosser or your whiskers are liable to fall off. Now – how about the loan?

LOBEY: Ah hivnae goat ten dollars tae gie ye an that's the truth. Ah had Elfie shod this mornin – cannae hiv her gallopin aboot in her berr feet in this weather. Nice shoes they are . . .

RANK: Sling backs?

LOBEY: Naw – bit ah had a guid mind tae sling them back when he tell't me the price o them. Things is terrible. Ah jist cannae gie ye the money.

RANK: Very well then – I shall hold up the Wells Fargo mail coach. Good day! (RANK BAJIN *starts to walk off*)

LOBEY: Jist a minit! Wait! Where's ma magic horse-shoe? (RANK *come back as* LOBEY *searches in his drawer, and produces the shoe.*) Ah'll gie it a bit rub an Fairy Nuff will appear wi her magic wand. She'll lend ye the money. (LOBEY *rubs his shoe;* FAIRY NUFF *appears.*)

FAIRY NUFF: On twinkling toes comes Fairy Nuff
      This wand o mine can do its stuff
      It will produce your heart's desire
      And if it don't then I'm a liar.

LOBEY: Any chance o a loan o ten dollars till next week hen?

FAIRY NUFF: Ten bucks? D'ye think ma heid buttons up the back Jimmy?

LOBEY: Hit's no fur me – hit's fur Bajin here. Ah'll gie ye it back next pay day.

RANK: I find myself, Miss Nuff, under some temporary financial embarrassment.

FAIRY NUFF:Your tail tis sad, does touch my heart
      Boo hoo boo hoo I'm wrenched apart
      Oh pray kind sir lend me your hankie
      This one I have with me is mankie.

RANK: Permit me madam . . . (BAJIN *gives* FAIRY NUFF *his hankie. She blows her nose loudly and tosses it back to him*)

FAIRY NUFF: Okay, then, here's my cheque for ten
> It is nae made of rubber
> If no repaid in seven days
> You'll both be in the grubber!

LOBEY: Thanks hen – yir a wee toff. (FAIRY NUFF *gives the cheque to* LOBEY, *although* BAJIN *has attempted to forestall her*)

RANK: My heartfelt thanks, Miss Nuff, and my warmest felicitations. I hope your mother is well.

LOBEY: (*To* BAJIN) Aw shut yer gob!

FAIRY NUFF: Goodbye, ta ta and toodle-oo,
> I've got tae scram tae Whiteinch noo
> Where I will meet my sister Mary.
> You see – she is the Yoker Ferry. (*exit* FAIRY NUFF)

LOBEY: Nice wee sowl, Fairy Nuff. Nae oil painting bit awfy guid-hertit. Noo – jist afore ah forget – whit are ye wanting the ten dollars for?

BAJIN: Well, you see, I have my poor old Mother to support at Westminster – she is a Lady MP and as if my cup of sorrow were not already full to overflowing, I find my bullet proof vest has more dents in it than the Government's reputation . . . (*Here* BAJIN *breaks down completely and collapses round* LOBEY's *neck.*) . . . But . . . thank God I am not too proud to beg.

LOBEY: There, there, there – nae need tae brek doon. Here's the cheque. (BAJIN *grabs the cheque with alacrity and instantly recovers his composure.*) An for guidness sake, Rank, try an dae better in future. Last week ye robbed Mrs Docherty's gas meter. The week afore ye liftit a bag o tattie crisps oot the Co. Ye canny carry on like that ye know. Ye'll end up in Barlinnie. Off ye go noo an try an turn a new leaf. (BAJIN *walks away slowly, then turns*)

BAJIN: Should I live to be a hundred, Dosser, I shall not forget your most generous financial assistance. I shall not forget it should I live to be two hundred. (BAJIN *exits*)

LOBEY: (*To himself – shaking his head*) Tut, tut, tut . . . an awfy man. Ah cannae help feelin sorry for him. He's aye been the same. When he wis wan year auld he used tae sit doon at the Barras in his pram, floggin his toys. Aw well ah'll get awa doon the toon the noo an check there's nae cheeky boys writin rude remarks aboot me on the walls.

(LOBEY *stands up and comes round from behind his desk, minus his pants. He looks down.*)

He's stole ma breeks!

BLACKOUT

In my time at the Citz I experienced many satisfying, dramatic and funny moments. Probably the most exciting episode for me was when I was cast as a wee sailor who was slightly 'under the influence.' The production was the Christmas Pantomime of 1951 – *The Happy Hap'ny*. Duncan Macrae had moved to the Alhambra and Stanley Baxter was the Dame.

The final Entire Company scene before the interval was set in Glasgow Central Station. The London train had just arrived and out poured a very mixed bag of travellers. Those involved included Joan Sims, John Fraser, Andrew Keir, Roddy McMillan, Madeleine Christie and Stanley Baxter as the star. Various different characters were represented : a very colourful American tourist, sporty types, business people and Stanley as a flashy, Joan Collins-type of film actress.

Each one or group acted out their contribution to the scene and moved off the stage. A loudspeaker announcement blared out and then receded in volume. Jimmy Gibson, as the ticket collector closed the gate and moved off on the prompt side. There was just the slightest musical hint of 'I Belong to Glasgow' and a wee sailor, complete with white scarf and small brown attaché case, opened the gate. I had been invited to write my own script. 'Aw hullo there Glesga! Ah'm hame!' I lurched to centre stage and stared up at the gods.

There was a cheer and a spontaneous round of applause.

'What a place! Ibrox Park, Lauder's Bar, The Shawfield Dugs, an' the jiggin'!'I did a mock waltz and a bigger cheer went up. 'Hullo there Ibrox Park ! Hullo 'there William Waddell ! Get in there boy, on the wing ! Give us the old Deedle Dawdell !' At that I shoogled my legs from side to side in my bell-bottom breeks and the audience seemed to go hysterical. They clapped, they whistled, they stamped their feet and cheered. At the end of my act I swayed off-stage and the curtain descended on the first half of the show.

Each night of the run the cheering for the wee sailor seemed to get louder. Needless to say, on Saturday nights, with many football supporters in the house, it was a thrill for me to feel the response.

Shortly before his death a couple of years ago I submitted some of my stories to my friend Archie P Lee, the BBC producer of the McFlannells. I had visited him in his home and we had been reminiscing about the Citizens' Theatre.

He wrote, 'You know Jimmy, I recall one Christmas Pantomime when you appeared as a wee sailor. You were in that state never described as drunk, but as "happy".' Then with an expression on your face which was a marvellous picture of admiration and hero worship you uttered the fervent words "Deedell Dawdell, William Waddell".' That is the impression that has lived with me all these years. The brief appearance you made on the stage is one of my unforgettable theatrical memories.'

Willie Waddell was the great Rangers hero at that time. He played on the right wing and will be remembered for his incredibly fast runs down the right wing before passing to Willie Thornton. His name has been commemorated in the Ibrox Waddell Suite.

Towards the end of the run of the pantomime I was informed that Willie himself was 'Out Front'– sitting in the front row of the dress circle. To be sure the wee sailor gave his act the full treatment that night. Shortly before his death I had the pleasure of meeting him for the first time and shaking hands with him at a Rangers FC Annual General Meeting.

He seemed frail and used a walking stick. I mentioned the Citizens' Theatre Pantomime of 1951. Alas – so much for hero worship – he had forgotten the night he went to the Citz and witnessed the famous 'Deedle Dawdell Shimmy Shoogle!'

FREELANCE

In 1950 I left the Citizens' Theatre and planned to spread my wings. London attracted me and I hoped that I might be able to obtain acting engagements in the theatre or in films. However, in the summer of that year my parents were spending a couple of weeks in Oban. On the final day of their holiday Mother became unwell and was admitted to Glasgow Royal Infirmary shortly after her return home. She was only in the infirmary for a few short days and died aged sixty-eight of peritonitis. I have the fondest memories of my mother. She was a gentle, loving and gracious lady. People used to say to her, 'My goodness, Mrs Stuart – none of your boys married yet? You must be too good to them!' They were right. Within three years of my mother's death, all four Stuart brothers were married.

The prospect of London would have to wait. I decided to stay in the family home and support my dad. By this time my three brothers had all left the nest.

The Stuart boys were spreading their wings. Jack, the eldest, did well at school. During the war he was commissioned in the RAF and served as navigator in Mosquito bombers. He chose the hotel business as his career, starting in the Central Hotel in Glasgow. While working as assistant manager at Gleneagles he met and fell in love with Margaret, the daughter of the Provost of Auchterarder. They were married in 1951 at Auchterarder and moved to Turnberry where he was now the manager. His work took him to hotels all over Scotland and the north of England. While working in the St Enoch Station Hotel in Glasgow (now demolished) he discovered three floors below ground level and the entrance to a nineteenth-century prison. How eerie it was to walk along the cobbled street and stand at the base of a spiral staircase looking out at the feet of passers-by rushing to Lewis's Department Store.

Like all three of my brothers, Jack was extremely artistic. His pencil drawing of my mother was striking in its classical simplicity. During his retirement, he moved to Kelso and his artistic focus fell on woodcarving, especially birds. These became so popular that at one point he had to stop supplying the National Trust Shop in Glasgow to concentrate on his local craft fairs where his carvings were in high demand. He died peacefully in 1997 aged eighty-two years. His wife Margaret, daughter Gaynor and son-in-law, John, survive him.

Next to fly the nest was Peter. He was an entirely different proposition from Jack. His horizons spread to the farthest corners of the globe, so as ship's carpenter he joined the Merchant Navy. His war was spent as a Petty Officer at the mercy of German submarines. His ship was bombed but he escaped unhurt. After the war when not at sea he worked in the shipyards as a joiner. Although this lacked the romantic appeal of life on the ocean wave, when you are working on what is to be the Royal Yacht there is a certain cachet. This did not dampen Peter's sense of fun. Noticing that my daughter Elizabeth had a packet of sweetie cigarettes that were very realistic, he borrowed them. Waiting until the foreman approached, Peter made a great show of hiding something behind his back. This naturally aroused suspicion. 'Stuart!' yelled the foreman, 'No smoking here.' 'Who sir, me sir?' Then bringing the offending object into view, he proceeded to eat it!

Just a note for future archaeologists if you ever have the chance to excavate a certain garden in Carntyne do not be surprised when you stumble upon an Aboriginal quern, some fool's gold and a supply of coral.

In the 1960s Peter followed our youngest brother to Canada. There he found the perfect occupation for himself as an appartments supervisor. His wood working skills, combined with his charm made him very popular. True to his career as a carpenter, Peter's artistic abilities were also with wood. His marquetry was beautiful. He married Gladys, a Canadian lass he met at a Burns Supper in Toronto and they lived happily together. Sadly he is now a widower but still enjoys his life in his adopted country.

Like Jack, Ron did well at school. When he left he worked as an electrician until he was called up in 1944. He was immediately recommended for a commission and was posted to India where he served as a Captain in the Royal Army Service Corps in Bangalore. On leaving the army he emigrated to Canada and like his brother Peter, he met and married a Canadian. Amy and Ron have been together now for forty-seven years. They have one son, John Ronald. He's married to Heather and they have two children, Andrew and Katie. Ron started work as a draughtsman with the Metropolitan Works department of Toronto and eventually became the manager of the Human Resources Department.

Ron is a first-class golfer and, following the Stuart tradition, he is a gifted wood carver and also accepts commissions as a sculptor. Ron is about to start writing his autobiography.

Where was I ? Oh, yes – freelance!

In 1951 the Citz recalled me on several occasions but in 1952 I took the plunge and headed for the bright lights of London. My good friend Archie Duncan from the Citz was making a name for himself in films and he kindly put me up in his flat. I walked for miles around the offices of theatrical agents and film casting places. When most of my money had run out I tried selling furniture polish from door to door. Alas – I did not sell one tin! For a few weeks I worked as a dishwasher at a Lyons restaurant, on the night shift from 10 p.m. till 6 am. My spirits rose when I did a tour of London schools with a small Shakespearean company presenting *Julius Caesar* and *A Midsummer Night's Dream*.

Here is a copy of a faded cutting, recalling my one and only West End Crit.

First Folio Theatre *Julius Caesar*

On May 17 as part of the Shakespeare Festival, 1952, the Southwark Borough Council presented the First Folio Theatre in *Julius Caesar* in the George Inn Yard, Southwark. James Stuart as Metellus Cimber swells his small part into an excitement of mighty sound, and his plea to Caesar at the Capitol exceeds the 'Will' scene in interest and anticipation.

When I returned home I joined the cast of TM Watson's popular comedy *Bachelors are Bold*. I had been offered a great part as Willie the milkboy. We toured Scottish towns and cities for three months with enormous success. That wasn't surprising as Duncan Macae was the star and he was in magnificent form.

I have a bright yellow and red theatre playbill in front of me. It states:

GAIETY THEATRE, KIRKGATE, LEITH

Twice Nightly, Week Commencing Monday, 2 March 1953.

FOR ONE WEEK ONLY

5 New Young Scots Comedians

Jimmy Neil

Jackie Wilson

Don Arol

Andy Stewart

Jimmy Stuart

All five were given equal size in billing space.

At that time Jimmy Neil was an established performer. For the other four aspiring comics it was their stand-up variety debut. Andy sang 'Ye Canny Shove Yer Grannie Aff A Bus', incorporating several different impersonations. It went well and of course he went on to international fame and popularity.

I gave a repeat of the 'Wee Sailor' act from the Citz panto and got a good response. The programme cost tuppence and the price of a seat in the stalls was two shillings. (10p)

In March 1954 I was one of a large cast in Walt Disney's film of *Rob Roy,* starring Richard Todd. It was shot in lovely spring weather in the Trossachs. We enjoyed five star service in the Baillie Nicol Jarvie Hotel. The midges were worrying but the money was good. It was a ten-week engagement. I was a Highlander one week and a Redcoat the next.

In the summer of that year I was contracted to top the bill in an English summer show in Swanage on the south coast. The show was called 'Each Evening – An Artistic Summer Entertainment Combining the Cheerfulness of Concert Party with the Sophistication of Modern Revue.' My blurb read as follows: 'Jimmy Stuart – a new young comedian of varied experience, who is already a successful cabaret artist and comes direct from an appearance in the film of *Rob Roy'*. On reflection I must have passed muster as a seaside entertainer as I did another season with 'Each Evening' the following year. The show ran for fourteen weeks each summer and was very well attended.

I continued to work as a freelance actor with the Citizens' Theatre, Dundee Rep and at Perth Theatre. Film and TV parts were in short supply but I managed to get a fair amount of broadcasting work from the BBC at Queen Margaret Drive.

AN ENGAGING EVENING

I KNOW FINE THAT I WAS always in love with May. As ten year-olds, we were both members of High Carntyne Church Sunday School and of the Junior Choir. We joined the Local Harriers – the CAAC (Carntyne Amateur Athletic Club) when it was formed in 1933. Fund-raising dances were held every Saturday night in the Co-operative halls in Pettigrew Street, Shettleston and I remember with pleasure making a sprint for May Kelt when a quickstep was called. She was a great wee birler! In my eyes she was the bonniest lass in Carntyne and my heart would beat faster every time I saw her. However there was no chance for Jimmy Stuart when the last waltz commenced and starry-eyed couples glided round the hall. That privilege always went to a tall, handsome redheaded lad called Duncan McVean – 'Doakie' to his friends.

Duncan and I were both members of the 162nd Company of the Boys' Brigade and were good pals. He worked, like his father, for the Stephen Mitchell Tobacco Company in Dunlop Street. As a youth he joined the Territorial Army and consequently, when war broke out in 1939, he was one of the first to be called up. We must now 'fast forward.'

At thirty years of age, I felt that I should really be thinking of settling down and perhaps even getting married but at the same time I was loth to part with my independence. I'd had a few brief friendships with girls but never any lasting relationships. May used to come round backstage when I was appearing at the Citizens' Theatre and as we lived near each other, we would return together on the bus to Carntyne.

During 1952 I had invited her to several theatre parties. At the beginning of 1953 our trysts seemed to become more frequent. At the end of March, on a Saturday, we attended a most enjoyable Citz Dance at the Central Hotel and returned home in a taxi in the wee sma' oors. I invited May in to have a coffee. My dad had retired to bed. I recall showing her some theatre photographs – probably trying to impress with my ham actor image. Needless to say, I had kissed girls before. As yet I had not kissed May. Why? Somehow the situation was different with May. Although to my knowledge she had no other attachment, she was a widow with a nine-year-old daughter and I guess I felt that advances should be sensitive.

Anyway – the night had gone well. May had met many of the well-known personalities. We had danced non-stop, we'd had a glass or two of wine and now were chatting away happily sitting on the sofa. Then I uttered a sentence. It was not in any way pre-meditated. I just said it. It was intended to be a kind of light conversational sentence. Really it was a sort of big deal of several staggered sentences.

'You know, May,' I mumbled, 'that was a super night we had tonight – sure was! Great night. Fair enjoyed it. And . . .' (there's a pause here – about five seconds.) 'Yes you know May – I want you to understand pal – I mean this sincerely – I don't consider this friendship of ours to be just a platonic affair.'

'Does that mean we're engaged?' says May. I don't pause for long. I daren't. I swallow. The inclination is to stutter. I speak clearly. 'Sure thing!' I reply. Then it happens and high time too, we have a cheeper. We got the ring and on 14 October 1953 we tied the knot in High Carntyne Parish Church, just two minutes from my home in Edinburgh Road.

After the ceremony in the church, my wife and I got into our taxi and were just about to drive away when we heard someone shouting. It was planned that Elizabeth should leave the church with her Aunt Margaret and Uncle Bill. In her excitement she couldn't find their car. So what does she do? In a panic she spots the bridal car and runs towards us. 'Mum! Mum! I can't find Auntie Margaret!' We open the door for her and the three of us drive away. I've only been married for twenty-five minutes and already I've a nine-year old daughter.

In my second year at Swanage, May decided to come down for the last performance as it fell on the Saturday of Glasgow's September weekend holiday. During the curtain call I announced to the audience that my new wife had just arrived from Glasgow, having walked the whole way. At the after-show party you can imagine May's surprise when people kept asking how long it took to walk from Glasgow.

KNOCK! KNOCK!

❁ ❁ ❁

AFTER GETTING MARRIED, I had to re-assess my situation. Living at home with my dad I could cope financially as a freelance actor. It was going to be a different story with a wife and daughter to support. May had stayed with her parents just round the corner from my house and we decided that she and Elizabeth would move into Edinburgh Road. It was now necessary to supplement my meagre earnings as an actor with some other income.

Seeing an advertisement for vacuum cleaner salesmen I decided to have a go. Anyone brave enough was welcomed with open arms into the situation. The basic wage was only £5 per week, so it was vital that sales were made. I was now living in the real world. However, May was working and I was determined that I was not going to sign on at the Labour Exchange. Even an unemployed actor has his pride!

I soon learned that if I could make a success as a vac sales-man, I could easily combine the job with acting opportunities when they came along. The vac firm was not concerned if one left the job for a month or more and then returned to it. As long as their product was sold, they were happy. So for a period of about four years I did both jobs; frequently knocking on doors by day and treading the boards or broadcasting in the evening.

In 1953, people had recovered somewhat from the war and most families had carpets in their home. Vacuum cleaners were not a new invention but were not manufactured during the war, so there was a ripe door to door market. All right, so how do you flog – sorry – how do you sell a vacuum cleaner?

Well it ain't easy, but if you're desperate and have a brass neck, it's amazing what can be achieved. I was desperate. I soon cultivated the brass neck.

We travelled in a small mini van from Glasgow City Centre, half a dozen salesmen, the driver/supervisor plus twenty boxed cleaners. We would descend on any part of a town or village , spread ourselves out and knock on doors. It's called 'cold canvassing.'

The procedure is to knock on the door and interview the householder. 'Hullo! Good morning! We're in the district all this week giving free demonstrations of our vacuum cleaners. Can I ask if you have a cleaner in the house?' Generally speaking, it's important to demonstrate only when the husband and wife are both present. A salesman knocks on a whole street of doors and hopefully lays on several 'dems' say to be given at 3 pm, 4 pm and 5 pm. In my time, I averaged about ten sales per week in a 5 day week. The commission for each sale was £3.

Now then – let's get down to the nitty-gritty! How is the sale made? First things first. You have to believe that you are going to make a sale. The procedure is in three parts as follows:

1.   Sell yourself
2.   Demonstrate the efficiency of the product.
3.   Close the sale.

Each part is vital to a successful sale.

PART ONE: *Sell yourself*
You must smile. You must be courteous. Crack a joke or two. You must be able to enter into any kind of conversation, in order to make the prospective customer feel at ease and give yourself a chance to present your spiel. Nine times out of ten the customer will say 'OK son, I'll take the demonstration, but I won't be buying.' That kind of remark should be ignored. However – let's suppose both husband and wife are in the house. You have patted the dog nicely, admired the wallpaper and complimented the husband on winning the

lovely trophy on top of the piano. Hopefully the atmosphere is friendly. You have sold yourself.

PART TWO: *The demonstration*

This part must be rehearsed at home just like a part in a play. The box is opened. The gleaming brand new cleaner is put on show. Let's assume that Mr and Mrs Smith do not own a cleaner. The salesman keeps talking while making a good job of cleaning the precious carpet. Without intending to cause embarrassment, an old newspaper is requested and the contents of the bag are emptied out. Shock! Horror! Disbelief! The husband gently chides his missus 'Oh! Goodness gracious! Tut,tut. Dearie me! My conscience.' Or words to that effect. 'Ah didnae think ye had as much muck as that on the flair!' The value of all the extra tools are now shown and the need for the product is demonstrated in a positive fashion. After a satisfactory demonstration there is not the slightest doubt in the minds of Mr and Mrs Smith that they do in fact *need* a cleaner. Getting them to make the decision to purchase is a different kettle of fish.

PART THREE: *Closing the sale*

It was never my practice to force a sale on anyone who could not afford to buy. I always checked on the circumstances of the prospective purchaser, made sure the husband was in work and observed the state of the house. My conscience was clear in that I was intending to sell something beneficial to good health. Nevertheless, closing the sale is the most delicate part of the deal and requires finesse and a steady nerve. In parts one and two there would be interesting presentations with plenty of eye contact. In part three – no eye contact! Why? I guess it's really psychological. Without any words being spoken the husband is usually miming to his wife, 'No! No! No!' and the wife is miming 'Yes! Yes! Yes!' Who would want to embarrass this nice couple by noting what was going on? It's best to keep the eyes down and produce the contract. Most people find it very difficult to make decisions.

A successful salesman must aid the customer by making the decision for them. 'Well, Mr Smith, I can see you're most satisfied with the cleaner. Now listen to this. That is a brand new cleaner that you saw me unpack. I'm happy to say that I can leave it with you right now. It's yours, Sir. The only deposit I require is £5 and the rest can be spread over a nine-month period, in easy payments and with a small credit charge.' The salesman places the credit sale agreement on the table and takes out his pen, remembering to avoid eye contact. 'What's the full address here, Mr Smith?' When Mr Smith gives the answer to the request for the full address, he has decided to buy! 'I'll give you a wee receipt for the £5 deposit. Just sign right there, Mr Smith. It's been a pleasure to meet you. I'm sure you'll be pleased with the cleaner.'

With belief in oneself and concentration, the actual 'execution' of a sale was not too difficult. Often it was dead easy; making a sale, meeting nice people and enjoying a cup of tea. The scunner of the job was in seeking out the prospective customers and arranging for the demonstrations. I have experienced days when I would knock on over three hundred doors – in the rain – and fail to be successful in arranging even one demonstration.

Was I unhappy? Well, I wasn't full of the joys of spring, but it was a job and I counted my blessings. I loved my wife and daughter. They loved me. I enjoyed good health and I was always optimistic that there would be good times ahead. I prayed. I sure did pray. Walking along the streets I would say 'Lord – you must know that I don't feel madly fulfilled wearing my knuckles away knocking doors. Please let it be that someday I can be used by you and feel satisfied in serving you.' I was prepared to be patient.

Most actors have periods when they are temporarily unemployed. It's called 'resting.' I had my share of rest periods. During one of them I saw an advertisement for quarrymen in the East End of the City where the Easterhouse Housing Scheme now stands. I made my way to the quarry and was directed to the foreman on the site. He was Irish, friendly, burly and about six feet six inches tall. I smiled nicely and told him that I was interested in the advertised job. He asked to see my hands, with palms facing upwards. That did it! He could see that I had never done a hard day's slog in my life. However, in my naiveté, when I realised why the Irishman had asked to see my palms, I could have told him I worked hard in my garden!

❂ ❂ ❂

BIG BREAK IN BARRA

❂ ❂ ❂

MINE WAS NOT A STARRING ROLE. But I was in the film and the BBC still screens it frequently. *Rockets Galore*, a follow up to Compton McKenzie's *Whisky Galore*, it was a gentle comedy about the efforts of a group of Hebridean Islanders to thwart the installation of a rocket range on their doorstep. Duncan Macrae played Duncan Ban, one of a quaint assortment of locals whose machinations and exploits held the plot together. The film was made on the lovely island of Barra, off the West Coast of Scotland. Most of the cast lived in cottages as guests of the local crofters. Ronnie Corbett (of the 'Two Ronnies' fame) and Duncan Macrae spent a lot of time, as a diversion, heaving huge boulders to one another.

I flew to Barra in June 1958 and met up with several of the famous personalities on the set: Jeannie Carson (singing star of many British musicals) Gordon Jackson (the well-loved butler from 'Upstairs Downstairs') and two fine Glasgow actors, Jameson Clark and Jimmy Copeland. I had only one line in the film but it was a big deal for me I assure you and I earned £150. Let me set the scene for my appearance: John Lawrie (Fraser from 'Dad's Army') is the Captain of the ferry and on arrival at the pier mutters 'Weel then, that wis a gey stormy voyage!' On the bridge as first mate I reply, 'Aye it wis thanks to you and God Almighty that we got here at all Captain!' Laurie sticks out his chest. 'Aye – two ferry guid men!'

Arriving on the beautiful sandy beach which served as the airstrip I was welcomed by my friend Duncan Macrae. He put me at my ease straight away. 'Jimmy, you'll probably not be called until tomorrow,' he informed me. 'Now then, wee man – d'ye see that bloody big hill behind the hotel? Later on tonight I want you to run like the clappers to the top and back. We'll give you a marked chuckie to leave at the top to prove that you got there. Jimmy Copeland has a stopwatch to time you. By jings! I'm depending on you son. You've got to beat the Englishman!' On that note he was called to meet with the director and left me wondering what on earth he was on about. Jimmy Copeland explained: the unit's favourite entertainment was spectating at the regular hill race between Macrae and Donald Sinden, as they competed with each other to cut down the time it took to run from the Castlebay Hotel to the top of a nearby hill and back. Sinden held the record of one hour and ten minutes. Macrae was a great Scottish Nationalist and had a bee in his bunnet from time to time about the English. Macrae seemed scunnered with Sinden's boasting each morning at breakfast about beating him. Although I remembered Donald Sinden as a courteous and friendly gentleman, how could I refuse the challenge?

I decided to forego dinner at 7pm and ordered some scrambled eggs on toast. Two hours later the Scots contingent waved me off and fifty-five minutes later I sprinted back to the starting line. Macrae was jubilant. With his usual flamboyance he waited until he spied Donald Sinden entering the hotel lounge before ordering champagne. Then, to complete his satisfaction he sent for the visitor's book.On the back page of the book, in big capital letters he wrote:

> *On this day 23 June 1958 Donald Sinden's record of one hour and ten minutes was smashed by Jimmy Stuart with a time of fifty-five minutes. Scotland Forever!*

I understand the incident is mentioned in Donald Sinden's autobiography.

❦❦❦

A STEPEK MANAGER

❦❦❦

In 1962 MY WIFE AND I had a conference. Life was good. We were very happy. Elizabeth was twenty-two years old and studying to be a teacher; May and I were blessed when we gave her a sister – Fiona – for company in 1958. We were all in good health and praised the Lord for His goodness.

My father had died on 19 December 1959. He was seventy-six years of age and died peacefully in our home. I know nothing of my dad's early life in the Isle of Mull before he came to Glasgow. This may surprise my family. It doesn't worry me. He was a loving, honest, hard-working husband and a devoted father to his four sons. I loved him dearly.

The time had now come for me to assess my future as an actor-cum-door-to-door salesman. To make a reasonable income as an actor in Scotland one has to possess more than just an average talent. May had never been in love with the so-called glamour of the show-biz life and I had tired of being away from home when a contract was offered outside Glasgow. We both agreed that a nine-to-five job in the city would be a happier occupation. I had no regrets and had learned the skill of acting. It was to prove useful.

A shop manager friend of mine happened to mention to me that his employer was looking for a manager to open a new branch of his television business in Burnbank near Hamilton. Was I interested? 'Yes please,' I said. In due course I was introduced to Mr Jan Stepek and he more or less said, 'Let me take you away from all this, Mr Stuart!' Over the next ten years, at different periods, I was the manager of nine of Mr Stepek's shops in Burnbank, Burnside, Hamilton,

Motherwell, Bellshill, Airdrie, Uddingston, Lanark and Blantyre. In my time I had the highest record of sales, so my door-to door selling had not been in vain.

Mr Stepek was a great boss and a tremendous inspiration to me. I can't understand why he hasn't been chosen for the BBC's 'This is Your Life.' He was born in Poland in 1922 and when the Germans and Russians invaded his country in 1939 he and his family were sent by cattle truck to a slave labour camp in Siberia. Released when the Soviets joined the Allies he spent six months in a Teheran hospital with malaria. He joined the navy and spent the rest of the war on convoy escort in the Mediterranean. Demobbed in 1945, he arrived in Glasgow and married Teresa Murphy. He opened his first shop in 1951, in Cambuslang, selling radios and records. They soon branched out into the television business. J Stepek Ltd now has twenty-one shops and eight travel agencies. Mr and Mrs Stepek have two daughters and eight sons who run the company, arriving at head office each day at 7.30 am. The Boss retired in 1982.

When Hamilton Accies Football Club was having financial problems Jan Stepek came to the rescue and was chairman of the club for twenty years. He never played football but he's a champion on the golf course and has seven holes in one to his credit.

Jan Stepek has been actively involved in promoting trade with Poland and has been honoured with the Commander's Cross and the Golden Order of Merit. He was awarded an Honorary Doctorate by the University of Strathclyde and a similar Doctorate from the University of Glasgow. In 1998 he was appointed honorary consul for Poland.

BACK-BREAKER

IN 1972 I WAS TEMPTED to try another job away from the electrical line and answered an advertisement for a job in a high-class furniture store in the centre of Glasgow. The pay offered was most attractive. I got the job and stuck with it for two years, selling three-piece suites, bedroom suites, dining room items, mirrors and pictures. It certainly was a change of routine, but the pressure remained. One had to graft for business to earn a decent commission on sales. However, the main drawback of the job, for me, was the physical effort demanded of the sales staff. The firm was loth to employ a sufficient number of porters to move the furniture from the store to the delivery vans; consequently the salesmen were obliged to manhandle their own particular sales. This often meant helping to lift heavy, tall wardrobes or beds and as I'm only a wee chap I wondered how long my poor back would stand the strain.

In the summer of 1974 I was most unhappy with my lot and felt that I really could not continue selling furniture. What did I do? I got down on my knees in my bedroom one night and spoke earnestly to my Maker: 'Lord, I'm sorry to say that I've got to get away from this big shop. Please, if you will, let it be that I can find some other way to earn a living.'

The following week I was made redundant. I was as happy as Larry. Not so my dear wife: 'What are you going to do? You're fifty-four years of age. Who's going to employ you?'

I tried to reassure May that I would find something, but she was very worried. As for me, I was honestly relieved to know that I would not be returning to the task of lugging heavy articles of furniture. Then began the chore of writing letters for jobs and visiting offices in the city asking about vacancies. I felt optimistic that my prayers would be answered. I figure there's not much point in praying unless one expects to have a positive response. Then something happened to convince me that my Heavenly Father has an enormous sense of humour.

On the Monday of my fourth 'idle' week, the phone rang. It was the manager of the shop where I had been employed. Surprisingly, business had picked up. Would I please return to the fold? It was good to know that I was wanted, but at the same time my heart sank, thinking about the weight of the wardrobes. 'Oh no! James, this is not happening,' I thought. 'What shall I say?' Feeling that, to an extent, I was in the driving seat, I asked if I could consider the offer and give my answer the next day. The manager was most amenable and said that he would look forward to hearing from me.

May worked as a shorthand typist in a city office. At 5.30 pm on that interesting day she returned home. 'Well Jamie – any good news today?' I informed her that the shop manager had invited me back to my old job. May's face lit up with joy and relief. 'Oh that's great, Jamie! Wonderful! Great news. When do you start back?'

I had the nerve to swallow a bit and appear to be totally in control of my destiny: 'I said I would think it over till tomorrow.' Well! It would be true to say that my darling wife nearly lost the heid an nae mistake! 'You said what, Jamie Stuart? You said what?' Then the tears began – but not for long. My loving partner took command of the situation. 'Are you out of your mind, Jamie? Promise me that you'll ring the shop in the morning and tell them that you'll start right away.' There was no point in arguing. May was right. I went back, albeit with a heavy heart and slipped back into the old routine.

However! Trust in the Lord! All was not lost. I had applied to Strathclyde Regional Council for a job in Social Work and seven days after re-starting my furniture job I was invited for an interview. I passed the interrogation successfully and was offered a post. I could start immediately. What absolute, utter, tremendous joy! Thanks a million, Lord!

It was with enormous satisfaction that I gave seven days notice to the shop. There were no hard feelings. They wished me well.

‡ ‡ ‡

SOCIAL WORK

‡ ‡ ‡

IN 1974 I JOINED THE Strathclyde Region Social Work Department as an RCCO (Residential Child Care Officer), based initially at Maryhill and then at Larchgrove, Edinburgh Road in the East End of the City. This appointment was to last until I retired aged sixty-five and gave me ten years of immense satisfaction and fulfilment. At long last I was really happy in my job. The routine of Social Work was entirely to my liking and met my need to do something worthwhile.

When I arrived at the Maryhill unit, on my first day, there were about thirty young lads in residence, ranging in age from about nine to sixteen years old. Their problems were varied: some had been bullied by their parents, some had been abused, others had been engaged in criminal acts such as housebreaking, shoplifting, mugging and car theft. Drink, drugs and glue-sniffing were big problems. The 1970s saw the emergence of the new profession of social work. As society became more complex, but also more compassionate, various programmes were developed to help those in need. There was a rapid expansion in job opportunities and these attracted mature people who could bring understanding as well as practical life experience to the job.

Scotland's radical children's hearing system, which sees young people in trouble as in need of help, guidance, education and support appealed to me very much. I saw the opportunity to work for welfare rather than punishment. Assessment centres had been established to replace remand homes – places aiming to determine not only why the youngsters were in trouble but also how they could be helped.

The Children's Panel would order a boy or girl to attend or stay in an assessment centre for three weeks or longer if more investigation or support was necessary.

I have before me a profile of myself written by my senior social worker in 1975: 'The boys who came to the centre where Jimmy Stuart began his career were upset, confused and suspicious of adults. And what about 'auld Jimmy'? – what did he know? Well he certainly knew the importance of fun and laughter. He was someone who would take an interest in you. Make sure you were clean and tidy and well fed. Riotous laughter could be heard as Jimmy embarked on an impromptu song and dance routine or a joke-telling session. Indeed colleagues would often remark at the end of an evening: 'The boys were fine, but see that man Stuart!' His old skills as an actor and salesman were put to good use. Some of the boys had tragic backgrounds with little or no family support. Bumped from children's home to foster home and on a constant not-so-merry-go-round, their behaviour deteriorated until they ended up stuck in an assessment centre with nowhere to go and facing a bleak future.

'Jimmy had a particular interest in these boys and one summer organised a week's holiday for them in Blackpool at the Glasgow Fair. He persuaded the manager of the Pleasure Beach to part with free vouchers for the carnival roundabouts and the lads had a ball. Of course no holiday would be complete without a visit to a posh hotel. How could Jimmy pull this off? Well, he did – that was the easy bit – the hard part would be ensuring that the boys behaved especially, when it was discovered they could use the swimming pool. Jimmy remembered the story that the English comedienne Dora Bryan told about her naughty small son 'performing' from the high diving board! He gathered his team around him and with a serious face explained that this was a modern hotel with all the latest technology including a 'pee-meter,' which set off a loud alarm if there were any 'accidents' in the pool. These lads were all street-wise, but surprisingly enough they actually

believed Jimmy's warning and obediently visited the facilities before entering the pool.

'It's never too late to go back to school. Jimmy was determined to make a career as a social worker, wanting to be better at helping those in need. At long last, attending night school, he passed his higher grade English exams and then began a course of study which would last almost three years to gain the certificate in Social Studies, one of the oldest successful students in the United Kingdom.'

One of the boys I had to deal with was Charlie. Charlie was fifteen years of age and six feet tall. He had the mental development of a ten year-old, had to be treated like a child and humoured a lot when he got out of hand. Referred to the police by his parents, he was being assessed because of his habit of shoplifting and bag snatching. Most of the time he was well behaved, accepted discipline and giggled a lot. I had a good relationship with big Charlie and when he was depressed I would take him for a walk on the football pitch and recite daft poems or sing 'The Wee Cock Sparra'. He seemed to like me. As events transpired I was thankful that we could communicate.

The drama happened on a Saturday morning. Most of the boys had been granted weekend leave. Charlie's leave had been denied because of unruly behaviour. To say that Charlie was unhappy would be an understatement. He was bitterly angry – left the dormitory and quite slowly and deliberately – began to hurl bricks at the school windows. He smashed about thirty of them. Taking my life in my hands, I ventured into the yard to confront our rebel. Seeing me coming, he picked up a very heavy rusty chain, began swinging it wildly and warned me not to come near. In the corridor, the staff held their breath. Like a brave movie star, I walk slowly forward. 'Don't come near, auld Jimmy – ah'll hit ye!' I get nearer and nearer. The nasty chain continues to swish ominously. 'Jimmy – ah tellt ye,'says Charlie. I now move straight into the danger zone – the chain strikes my shoulder (it doesn't hurt me in the slightest) – I scream out in agony and like the awful corny actor I am, begin to bawl and cry like a baby. Charlie drops the chain, puts his arms round my shoulder and begins to weep in company with me. Sobbing pathetically together, we proceed to the dormitory, have a Coca-Cola and a game of table tennis.

A SEED IS SOWN

◔◔◔

In September 1981, I paid a visit to the Edinburgh International Festival and witnessed an acclaimed one-man dramatic presentation by Alec McCowen. The English West End actor had memorised the whole of Mark's Gospel from the King James Version of the Bible. His performance was sensational. He played to packed houses and received standing ovations. This presentation by McCowen had a significant impact on my life and triggered off a remarkable sequence of events, which, in my wildest dreams, I could never have imagined happening to me.

Returning home in the train between Waverley Station and Queen Street, my wee head was bursting with a plan. I felt the urge to emulate McCowen's feat in some way. I believe that if we have a worthwhile talent, then we should use it for personal fulfilment and also, hopefully, to please or inspire other people.

'Right then, James,' says I to myself, 'you're inspired by McCowen. What can you do about it?' McCowen had recounted the Gospel in the English language. I could tell the story in the Guid Scots tongue! I had a fair idea it had never been done before in an acting format and from my experience as a professional actor in the Glasgow Citizens' Theatre I had acquired a good working knowledge of the Scots language. I remembered that I had a copy of *The Four Gospels in Braid Scots* written by the Reverend William Wye Smith and published way back in 1901. I contacted the publishers and was given permission to adapt the work for dramatic presentation. This did not work out very well and I decided to go it alone. Over a period of two years I combined the four gospels of Matthew, Mark, Luke and John into one single narrative, had all the hand written pages typed out and memorised the script. My own minister at High Carntyne Church, the Reverend James Martin invited me to present a short passage of the work during a Sunday morning service in our kirk. It seemed to meet with approval. I was encouraged.

In the autumn of 1982, I journeyed to Edinburgh with a view to speaking to the Church of Scotland Director of the Netherbow Arts Centre. Some years before, I had broadcast with the Reverend James Dey at the BBC in Glasgow and I reckoned that he might give me some guidance. The Netherbow is annexed to John Knox House in the cobbled High Street. On arrival I was welcomed by a tall, bearded young man who informed me that Mr Dey was on holiday. 'Oh right,'I said. 'Many thanks, I'll call again.' I turned to head for the door. I expect the young man was curious. He certainly was very friendly. 'Can I be of any help?' he volunteered. That meeting is fixed in my memory. My immediate reaction was a feeling of embarrassment. Was I prepared to pour out my ideas to a total stranger and risk a dent to my enthusiasm?

'I wanted to ask Mr Dey for some advice about some writing,' I answered. 'I'm an elder in High Carntyne Church in Glasgow. I used to do a bit of acting and I thought of presenting the gospel story in dramatic form – in the Guid Scots tongue!' The good Lord sure works in wonderful and unexpected ways. The young man was Dr Donald Smith and at that time he was the Assistant Director at the Netherbow. 'Tell me more,' he said. 'It might interest you to know that I took my doctorate in the Scots language at Edinburgh University. It seems like a great idea. Why don't I take you down to our wee theatre downstairs? Can I hear some of the piece?'

We made our way down to the theatre and I presented the Good Samaritan and the Prodigal Son. From that moment my project really took off. The Reverend James Dey moved on some months later and Donald Smith took control of the Netherbow. He suggested that I call my effort *A Scots Gospel* and offered to help me. Thereafter I made several monthly visits to Edinburgh and Donald edited the entire work.

Prior to seeing Alec McCowen in 1981, I had never really done any serious writing so this was an exciting and fulfilling experience for me. May was not at all sure that there was any real worth in what I was trying to do, nonetheless she supported me in every possible way and wished me well.

When May and I married in 1953 we were both smokers. At forty years of age, I stopped and smugly felt that everyone else in the world should do the same. May was not a heavy smoker and I did all in my power to persuade her to stop. She knew that cigarettes were bad news but felt powerless to give them up. She even tried help from a hypnotist, with no success.

Early in 1981, May had her first heart attack. Her doctor advised her to give up smoking, saying that though it would not guarantee that she did not have another heart attack – if she did not stop there and then, that she would die. My dear wife took the advice and stopped smoking.

In January 1983 she had another heart attack. It hurts me to hear any criticism of the staff at Glasgow's Royal Infirmary. The doctors and nurses were magnificent in their kindness and care. May died peacefully aged sixty-one in the evening of February 9, 1983. We had enjoyed thirty years of loyal happy union.

I cannot find the words to describe my feelings when May went out of my life. I did a lot of praying and I know my prayers were answered. God promises strength and comfort to believers. It now seemed to me that writing was going to be my salvation.

❦❦❦

THE MARATHON

❦❦❦

DURING THE 1970S THERE AROSE a big interest in marathon running which seemed to climax around 1980. In the USA thousands of athletes and untrained optimists all wanted to experience the great ego trip and casually boast of winning a marathon medal. Everyone who completed the distance received a medal.

There is a kind of fascination about the marathon – the classic running event of 26 miles, 385 yards. It's recognised as a test of great endurance. The name stems from the legend of a battle near the Greek town of Marathon in 490BC. The Athenians were victorious over the Persian Army and a Greek soldier named Pheidippides was directed to take the news of the success to Athens. He ran the twenty-two miles from the battlefield, arrived in Athens, shouted 'Rejoice, we conquer!' and, sadly, fell down and died.

Chris Brasher, the English athlete and former Olympic Steeplechase champion, organised the first London Marathon in 1981. I was caught up in all the *brouhaha* and in 1982 (at sixty-one years of age) I entered and completed the London Marathon. Later the same year I finished the first Glasgow Marathon with my best time of three hours and fifty-nine minutes. It's exhilarating to be involved in the excitement and camaraderie of the event and I was pleased to raise some money for Christian Aid and Save the Children.

Like most competitors in the marathon, I 'hit the wall'. Marathon runners have long recognised that there comes a point in the later stages of the race, usually between eighteen and twenty-three miles, when running suddenly becomes very much harder. Suddenly, without warning, the runner is dragged down to a much slower pace, despite increased effort. Weak legs, acute muscle discomfort and fatigue, together with severe doubts about even completing the distance accompany the change. The sensation is commonly known as 'hitting the wall', because that is what it feels like.

After approximately eighteen miles of hard running, the muscles have used up their chief energy-providing source, glycogen (which is stored carbohydrate in the form of sugar) and a chain reaction sets in as new stocks of fuel are urgently sought by the muscles. The body switches to using fat for fuel. This, although readily available, is a less efficient alternative. I 'hit the wall twice' but managed to run through it and finished in one piece, tired but elated. I could have cried with joy – and later on I did in fact shed tears. In emotional circumstances I don't think it's surprising that grown men cry. God gave us the ability to bring on helpful tears when they are required. What sports follower will ever forget the amazing sight of the former Rangers and England football star, Paul Gascoigne, weeping buckets on the field when England were defeated during the 1990 World Cup? Towards the end of his running career, Steve Ovett and his fellow Olympian, Sebastian Coe, were set up together in a very emotional mile race duel. The race organisers had misled Ovett about the conditions of the event and after the race in a television interview he wept uncontrollably.

In September 1982, I was in Church one Sunday morning sitting quietly. The Minister was reading the intimations when I suddenly heard my name being mentioned. 'And now, friends, we have a surprise for our Elder James Stuart. After his success in the London Marathon earlier this year and the Glasgow Marathon last week, I can reveal that Christian Aid has benefited from his efforts.' I was signalled to come forward. 'James – we would like you to accept this trophy to mark your achievements.'

I collected my reward and, as I returned to my seat, unashamedly enjoyed a nice wee bubble.

A SCOTS GOSPEL

In the autumn of 1983 I found solace from my grief at losing May when I joined my minister the Reverend James Martin and his group on a visit to the Holy Land. It was an unforgettable experience.

On the first day our coach took us to Bethlehem. Leaving Jerusalem we passed places which were to become landmarks during our stay in the area: Gethsemane, Lion's Gate and St Andrew's Church. We visited the Shepherds' Fields where it is reckoned that the shepherds saw the angel telling them of Christ's birth. There has been a church on this site since the fourth century.

Arriving at the Church of the Nativity in Manger Square right in the heart of Bethlehem, we entered by the door where every person must bend the head to view the birthplace of our Lord.

Returning to Jerusalem we headed for St Stephen's Gate to begin our first visit to the Old City. The walls of the city have been rebuilt sixteen times.

We travelled to the lowest spot on the surface of the earth and some of us floated in the buoyant waters of the Dead Sea where the salt content is in the region of 26%. Our minister lay on his back in six feet of water and read a newspaper.

A few miles from the Dead Sea we saw the spectacular Rock of Masada which is one thousand feet high and I remembered reading about Herod's great palace built on top of the Mountain. In 70AD 980 Jews escaped from the Romans in Jerusalem and fled to the safety of Masada. The Romans followed determined to capture the stronghold. For three years as many as ten thousand Roman soldiers camped at the base of the mountain. They built a ramp and eventually reached the summit of Masada. Breaking through the barricades they were met with a great silence, for the Jews had chosen suicide rather than capture. Most visitors make the one thousand foot ascent to the summit by cable car. As I was in training for another marathon, I spotted the snaking path and jogged to the summit and back. I was given a certificate and T-shirt from Mr Martin – 'Conqueror of Masada'.

I have a cherished memory of the time when we arrived in Tiberias. On a lovely still cool evening, just as the sun was setting, I gave my first public reading of *A Scots Gospel* to our group. The reading took place on the roof garden of the Church of Scotland Centre overlooking the Sea of Galilee.

Although I was presenting the Gospel, I felt that our group was involved in the story-telling. It was a joyful feeling. Somehow, on that night, it seemed to me that everyone in the entire world was happy and at peace with their neighbours.

It was refreshing indeed to take part in the pilgrimage/holiday to the Holy Land, as I endeavoured to come to terms with life without May. Sadly, my wee family suffered another crushing blow on my return in September.

Weir Pumps of Cathcart had employed my son-in-law Iain for all his working life. He married my daughter Elizabeth in 1968 and their only child Kirsty was born in 1976. Although Iain had leukaemia for most of his adult life, it was not until 1983 that the condition became acute. His health deteriorated during the summer of 1983 and he died in the Victoria Infirmary on 11 October 1983, aged only forty-one.

Iain Harvie was a kind, loving husband and father. He was a small man – like myself – just five feet five inches tall, but his stature didn't affect his abilities in so many directions. He was a first-class engineer, mechanic and joiner. It was always his ambition to sail his own boat and he worked hard to make this dream come true. He and Elizabeth owned their own folkboat – *Polka* – and berthed it first at Rosneath and then at Gourock; the three of them enjoyed several happy summers sailing to Rothesay, Ardentinny and Tarbet.

In 1985 Donald Smith arranged a tour of churches, schools, theatres and prisons throughout Scotland for me to give my one-man dramatic presentation of *A Scots Gospel*. I had memorised everything but usually placed the manuscript on a lectern in case of emergency. The presentation was in two parts, each fifty minutes long with a twenty-minute interval.

In the autumn of 1985 my friend the Reverend Jim Martin (no relation to my own minister) formerly of Kilsyth Congregational Church and now an international evangelist, contacted his brother the Reverend Robert Martin in Canada to set up a tour of churches in North Ontario. Rob Martin put me up in his lovely country home in Vankleek Hill and arranged everything. My first appearance was a safe one, to the ladies of the Women's Guild. Bless the ladies. In Canada, as in Scotland, they are the backbone of the Church. All went well. Performances were given in Presbyterian churches in Hawkesbury, Vankleek Hill, Lancaster, Howick, Kempville, Finch and Ottawa.

During the General Assembly of The Church of Scotland in 1985, the church and nation committee said that our people should give more thought to the Scots language. I'm pleased to report that the Scots-Canadians I met on my tour have a great love of their Scottish heritage and culture. The response by Scots, Canadians and others to the story of Jesus told in the Scots language was similar to the reactions I had experienced in Scotland. At the receptions after the performances I met Scots from Aberdeen, Ayr, Kilmarnock, Edinburgh and Glasgow. Some of them had emigrated a long time ago and had never returned to visit the land of their birth. They were filled with emotion to hear the familiar Bible stories told in their ain guid Scots tongue. In my travels one lady was fair chuffed to hear me declare 'Let us eat and be blythe, for ma son wis deid an cam back tae life once mair: he has been tint an is fund.' She had memorised the wording on an old sundial near her home: 'Tak tent o time, ere time be tint (*lost*).'

🦁🦁🦁

PAPER BOY

🦁🦁🦁

I HAVE USUALLY BEEN fortunate with the regularity of my morning newspaper deliveries. However in December 1988 my boy 'retired' and my newsagent was finding it extremely difficult to do the run for Edinburgh Road. After complaining about not getting my *Herald* delivered, I jokingly said to the lady manager that I felt like offering myself for the job. She was at the receiving end of a lot of hassle from the customers: 'Mr Stuart, I hope you're not kidding, that would be great! When can you start?' On an impulse I told her that I'd be at the shop at 6 am the following day.

I left the shop in a daze. My only worry now was how my school teacher daughters would react to my going back to work aged sixty-eight. When my younger daughter Fiona arrived home from work I told her of my morning job. 'Ha! Ha! Very funny, Dad!' She laughed. Then it dawned on her that her eccentric old dad was serious. 'My goodness, the neighbours will think you're doing it for the money.' The pay was £9 per week!

As promised, I reported on time the next day and continued the job for six months. I set my alarm for 5.30 am each day and got stuck into the idea of being a paper boy once again. As a boy I had delivered papers on the same route for four years, so I was turning back the clock just over fifty years. What an incredible experience it was. Thomas Carlisle wrote: 'Work is the grand cure for all the maladies and miseries that ever beset mankind.' He was so right. However, as a retired person I was not at all unhappy; on the contrary, I was living life to the full and here was a golden opportunity

to test my discipline at early rising. The shop employed another four paper boys; I mixed in with them and was accepted as one of the team.

In December and January we had some very heavy snow and I can remember at least two mornings when the hailstones seemed to batter through my balaclava, like pellets from an airgun. I worked out the shortest routes from door to door and vaulted over fences when the opportunity arose. Most of the time I jogged and the feeling of euphoria when I pushed the last *Herald* or *Record* through a letter box was a lovely experience. Breakfast was enjoyable as I felt that I had earned it.

When the spring arrived it was a joyous time to be bouncing up and down paths with my bag full of world and local news: good news, bad news, war, peace, scandal, sport, politics, personalities, programmes for the telly, forecasts, fashion, agony columns and articles for sale – all waiting to be digested by my readers. March and April were my favourite months. In the early morning there was little traffic. The smell of springtime at 6 am is enchanting. The birds seem to sing at their sweetest, the buds in the trees and shrubs are pulsating with life and of course the snowdrops and daffodils are wondrous to behold.

At the end of May, a wee lassie wanted the job. I hung up my bag. I was sorry to leave.

AUTHOR

AFTER I RETURNED HOME FROM CANADA, the Church of Scotland Pathway Productions Unit made an audio cassette of my theatrical performance. The next development floored me completely. Donald telephoned to inform me that Saint Andrew Press, the publishing arm of the Church of Scotland, wanted to publish *A Scots Gospel*. 'Come on Donald!' I said. 'You're joking! Publication? This is Jimmy Stuart you're talking to – repeated his second year at Whitehill School – sold vacuum cleaners door-to-door for four years! Are you serious, Donald? Will I be called an author?'

My wife May was the only person who ever called me Jamie. I had an idea. How could I make her a part of this new venture? *A Scots Gospel* by Jamie Stuart was launched in the Netherbow Arts Centre in Edinburgh on Tuesday 19 November, 1985. We received coverage on television, radio and in the press. The *Glasgow Herald* reported 'The well known story of Jesus of Nazareth is re-enacted in the gutsy vernacular of the Scots tongue – delightful and dramatic – it demands to be aired publicly, or read aloud around the family fire.'

Dr Donald Smith wrote the following introduction: 'Taken along with the development of the Glasgow Citizens' Theatre, the astonishing growth of the Scottish Community Drama Association and the foundation of the Edinburgh International Festival, the Edinburgh Gateway's twenty-one years of active existence are evidence not just of the renaissance in Scottish Theatre, but of a new alliance between church and theatre which was sealed by the triumphant production of Sir David Lindsay's sixteenth-century morality play *Ane Satyre of the Three Estaits* at the Edinburgh Festival in 1948. Directed by Tyrone Guthrie, the play was performed in the Church of Scotland Assembly Hall by a distinguished Scottish cast, which included the author of *A Scots Gospel*. This dramatisation of the Gospel story in colloquial Scots, conceived by a Scots actor, will certainly be enjoyed by audiences in churches and theatres alike.'

The John Knox Press of Atlanta in the USA published an American edition of *A Scots Gospel* with an all blue tartan style and with this introduction: 'For all who find roots or romance in Scotland, who delight in the sound of a broad Scots burr and the skirl of the pipes, who rejoice in the soft beauty of a tartan and the imposing dignity of a kilted Highlander, may your hearts be lifted up by hearing again, in this new way, the old, old, story of the life of our Lord among us.'

In the wake of *A Scots Gospel* a number of Glasgow ministers suggested to me that I should consider writing the Gospel stories in the Glasgow vernacular. I hesitated. Many people love the pithy, pungent patois of Glaswegians while many others have little regard for it. My good friend the Reverend John Campbell, the Church of Scotland Advisor on Mission and Evangelism encouraged me. 'Jamie – I'll tell you something,' he said, 'from time to time I pay a visit to the Barras on a Saturday morning with the express intention of listening to the Glasgow Patter. It's a real joy. Why shouldn't the greatest story ever told be presented in the language of the people? It's never been done before. Jesus must have conversed in the ordinary language of the people.'

During 1991 John Campbell called in to my home in Carntyne frequently and guided me in the intricate task of translating the Gospels into accessible and meaningful Glasgow-speak. Every big city has unpleasant slang terms of communication so it was important to avoid colloquial language with unacceptable words and usages.

The launch of *The Glasgow Gospel* was scheduled for 16 April 1992 in the Church of Scotland bookshop in Buchanan Street, Glasgow. On the previous Monday, the Church of Scotland issued a publicity release to Associated Press. It went round the world on 'the wire.' On the Tuesday the phone never stopped ringing. The BBC, ITV, Radio Scotland, Radio Clyde, Radio Wales, Radio Belfast and Toronto Radio all interviewed me by telephone. From the USA, Washington DC Radio wanted to speak with 'Mr Stoo-art.' The interview was broadcast coast to coast. Imagine the surprise of one of my friends who was cruising on the *Canberra* when she heard my voice coming from the radio. On the Wednesday morning I was awakened at 6 am by the phone ringing. It was a request for an interview with Melbourne Radio. Meanwhile in Glasgow, Radio Clyde was broadcasting an advertisement for the *Glasgow Evening Times* which was serialising chapters from the book – two whole centre page spreads, Monday to Friday – in colour.

In the Saint Andrew Press Office in Edinburgh they were getting some strange requests – a local kilt maker's order had to include six copies of *The Glasgow Gospel* for a customer in the USA. Also, on Easter Sunday, the lunchtime ITN news carried a feature on the Pope's address, a message from the Archbishop of Canterbury and Jamie Stuart with *The Glasgow Gospel*.

On the Thursday Lesley Duncan of the *Glasgow Herald* phoned me to request a copy of the book for reviewing on the Saturday. She couldn't get a copy in any of the shops as the first edition of 3,000 copies had sold out within hours. I took a copy to the *Herald* offices. Lesley Duncan interviewed me. In her review she wrote: 'Had I two minutes to spare? Of course I had. That is how I found myself listening, a transfixed audience of one, to the Parable of the Prodigal Son rendered in Glasgow patois. The reader was Jamie Stuart, seventy-one year-old elder of High Carntyne Church, whose paperback, *The Glasgow Gospel*, has propelled him into unexpected national celebrity this week.'

With all the *brouhaha* surrounding the publication of *The Glasgow Gospel* and seeing the wee book go to number one in the Scottish Bestsellers' List I thought it might be a good idea to exploit the interest and try to raise some money for a good cause. I asked the director of Save the Children if she would approve of the Church of Scotland making a video film of *The Glasgow Gospel* with profits going to the Save the Children charity. She was delighted to consent.

Laurence Wareing was in charge of Pathway Productions, the kirk's video units in Edinburgh. We knew each other well as he had produced my audio cassettes of *A Scots Gospel* and *The Glasgow Gospel*. I explained my idea to him over the phone and he came to my home to discuss the feasibility of filming the book. Laurence knew little about locations in Glasgow. 'Where would we make it, Jamie?' he asked. 'No trouble at all in that respect, Laurence,' I replied. 'We'll use Sauchiehall Street, Buchanan Street, Argyle Street, George Square, the City Chambers, the Royal Concert Hall, the People's Palace, the Museum of Transport, the Cathedral, Botanic Gardens – will I go on?' 'No, Mr Attenborough stop there! How do we get permission to film in these places?' I reminded him that Glasgow was the friendly city and that it was unlikely that we would find any difficulty with permits for shooting. Laurence was warming to the potential. 'All right, Sir Jamie, who's going to star in this epic production?' I was ready for this, 'Laurence, dear sir, this the easiest part of my whole idea. As an old has-been actor I am still in touch with personalities in the entertainment circle. I'll approach Eileen McCallum, Gwyneth Guthrie, Mary Marquis and Molly Weir. For the male roles I'll speak to Andy Cameron, Johnny Beattie, Tony Roper, Paul Young, Walter Carr, Alex McAvoy, Alastair McDonald and Peter Morrison.' Laurence was impressed. 'One wee point Jamie, how do we know these folk are going to work without any fee?' 'No headache here,' I assured him. 'If they're not prepared to give their time to Save the Children for free, then they don't take part.' There was little doubt in my mind that the aforementioned artists would be willing to co-operate if they were available.

I had the feeling that when Laurence came to see me that day in my house in Carntyne, he really intended to be polite, to listen to me and to tell me that my idea was too ambitious. As it turned out, we drank a lot of coffee and talked for three hours. The month was August. In order to set up the administration, approach the cast and plan to have the video on sale in the shops in November to catch the Christmas market, we realised we would only have two weeks to do the actual filming. It was going to be a tight schedule and the weather clerk would have to be kind to us. Alison Fleming started telephoning our chosen people. My good friend, Jimmy Black, author, poet and great authority on Glasgow, volunteered to take Laurence and his film crew on a reconnaissance of the city and some very interesting locations were identified. Permission was granted for all location filming and Stewart Black was commissioned to compose original theme music. Filming commenced on 6 October and was completed by 30 October. We were blessed with dry weather and all went well. Jimmy Black presented the Nativity Story from the Queen Mother's Hospital. The youngest member of the company was Amanda – just twenty-four hours old – who played the part of baby Jesus. She was brilliant and took direction without a murmur.

Andy Cameron delivered the parable of the Prodigal Son from Central Station and Johnny Beattie read Peter's Denial from the Italian Centre. Laurence didn't allow me to choose my own scenes, but I was not surprised to be cast as Zacchaeus. There is only one tree in Argyle Street. It's been there a long time and is regarded as a 'listed tree.' In *The Glasgow Gospel* does Zacchaeus actually climb the tree? Buy the video and you'll find out.

Alex McAvoy's depiction of the crucifixion filmed in the Necropolis was quiet and sensitive, while Mary Marquis' telling of the resurrection scene set in the Botanic Gardens was incredibly moving. To complete the cast I invited my elder daughter Elizabeth to take part and also the former director of the Citizens' Theatre, Lea Ashton. Last but not least, my friend the Reverend Jack Lamb presented the chapter on John the Baptist. Jack is now working as the minister at Townsend Road Presbyterian Church in Belfast, between the Shankhill Road and the Falls Road. I joined two busloads of supporters from Stirling attending his induction there.

The Glasgow Gospel is the Church of Scotland's best selling video and is still very popular. It has raised considerable funds for Save the Children.

One of the first people I invited to appear in the video was my good friend Alastair McDonald, the popular Scots folk singer. It was an inspired choice! Alastair became a Christian twenty years ago and since then has become a driving force in evangelism. Laurence Wareing wanted Alastair to be in the market place casting out the money-changers and pigeon-dealers. There was never any doubt about the most suitable location – Glasgow Barrowland – the Barras!

We set up one Sunday morning during the hustle and bustle of the market. Alastair was in dramatic mood: 'When Jesus went into the Temple he wis furious at whit he saw gaun oan. Barras everywhere – wheelin an dealin! At wance he heaved ower the tables o the money-chingers, an upset the stools o the pigeon-dealers, cryin oot; 'God said this Temple is for prayer an worship. You lot hiv turned it inty a den o cheats!'

Laurence finished the shot with Alastair but then panned the camera to the side where a young busker was playing his guitar and singing Bob Dylan's 'Knockin on Heaven's Door.' Did he get an answer to his knocking? This is Alastair's account of what happened on that Sunday and of a certain sequel:

'On the Sunday morning Laurence, Jamie and I met in the Barrowland office prior to going out on the shoot. It was agreed that a word of prayer would be in order. We prayed.

'Months later my wife and I were attending Spring Harvest, a Christian Festival held in Ayr when a young man approached me and said, "Hi, you and I appeared in a video together!" His face did appear to be kind of familiar although a good deal changed and he went on to explain. He had been busking on the street around the Barras to prop up a heroin addiction when a camera crew took a cut-away shot of him playing and moved on, an incident which he promptly forgot. Eventually the heroin led him into Barlinnie jail for petty theft and on Easter Sunday morning, for want of something better to do, he attended the service which included a showing of *The Glasgow Gospel* on a giant screen. There he was churning out "Knocking on Heaven's Door!" In addition to this the sermon included Pilate's words, ". . . it is within my power to release a prisoner unto you . . ." (John 18:39) On returning to his cell he was given the news that he was being released and this combination of astounding events led to some serious thought about himself, his situation, his responsibilities and above all, his deliverance. Today, free from both jail and heroin, he pursues Christian work in and out of prison – a walking testament to answered prayer. Unknown to the three men saying a vague 'Amen' in the Barrowland Offfice, God's answer was being poured down on the life of a street busker outside, some thirty yards away.'

After the publication of my wee book I received letters from all over the world. One letter from the USA was of particular interest. The Reverend George M Docherty, Maryhill-born and ordained in the Church of Scotland, wrote to congratulate me on my work. George's own story is well worth telling.

He was 'called' to America in 1950 and became a US citizen ten years later. It was thanks to him that the American Pledge of Allegiance contains the words 'Under God.' In his autobiography *I've seen the Day* George tells of discussing the pledge with his son while working on a sermon for his church in Washington DC. George suddenly realised that the pledge didn't have any reference to God in it and decided that he'd just found his sermon. The name of his church was the Church of the Presidents and one of his congregation happened to be the then US President Dwight Eisenhower.

The sermon was reported nationwide and provoked a flurry of support. As a result of all this, the words 'Under God' were officially inserted after the phrase 'one nation' in June 1954.

The Reverend Docherty was active in the US civil rights movement. He marched with Martin Luther King and opposed the Vietnam War. He was widowed in 1970 and remarried two years later at the age of sixty. Not only that, but he had two children in what he calls 'the autumn of my years.' I learned his story from the copy of his book that he kindly sent me. I am glad to say I've made a new friend.

☙ ☙ ☙

CARRYING THE CAN

☙ ☙ ☙

ONE SATURDAY AFTERNOON my conscience was troubling me. It was Cup Final day on the telly and also the final day of Christian Aid Week. Peggy, our indefatigable Christian Aid organiser, had paid her annual visits to the local pubs, clubs and shops and reported back to the church with heavy cans. Just back from five weeks holiday, I had done nothing to support the cause.

Rejecting the temptation to watch the game, I board a bus for Glasgow City Centre to do my wee bit to help the hungry folk of the world. It is smirring as I take up my position in Argyle Street. I use two cans to attract attention. Almost immediately a lady opens her purse and pops in a one pound coin. (Well that's a good start, Jamie!) A colourfully dressed young man and his girl partner are doing some expert juggling nearby and drawing a fair crowd. Their cardboard box is bulging with coins and paper money. A news vendor screams out the latest headlines and a large lady is doing a bomb with fresh strawberries. It is lunchtime and shoppers zigzag all round me. The drizzle is getting unpleasant. Having personally hanselled my two tins, I start gingerly to shake them and try to look relaxed. (Smile at no one in particular and hope for some eye contact.)

Fifteen minutes pass.

No further contributions.

Home beckons. (When does the game start?) Tut, tut Jamie. Don't be faint-hearted. How about Buchanan Street? Now, that must be Christian Aid territory. Opposite a famous

111

store in Buchanan Street a cheery accordion player squeezes out some popular melodies. The rain stops. The sun comes out. I jingle my cans in time with the music. A wee lassie comes tripping up and pops in half a dozen coins. 50p pieces and small change are all willingly donated. Here's a friendly officer of the law. 'Making out okay, Jimmy?'

'Aye, fine sergeant.' (How did he know my name?) Both cans are now full. I'm delighted. Yes indeed, life has meaning. God willing I'll be back on the same pitch next year.

There are thousands of charities around these days, all competing for our money. If we are caring people I reckon we should do what we can to help those in need. We often shy away because we read of so much misuse and fraud. Christian Aid and Save the Children are well-founded and reputable organisations.

In 1995 I had an entrepreneurial urge. I love that word. It sounds dramatic. John Smith, the Glasgow Chairman of Save the Children liked the suggestion that we should hold a Burns Supper in aid of Save the Children. We formed a small committee. The Hilton Hotel was booked for 26 January, 1996 and the planning began. My good friend David Hardman agreed to be Chairman at the Supper after I suggested that his car hire firm should subsidise the event to the tune of £5,000. He obliged. I invited Jimmie McGregor to present the Immortal Memory. Anne Linstrum, Alastair McDonald and Peter Morrison were the singers. Jimmy Black proposed the Toast to the Lassies and the Reverend Lorna Hood replied to it. My own party pieces completed the programme. It was a gey noisy supper. I wouldn't say that our guests were out of control. Let's state that they were decidedly fleein! Never mind – we raised £12,000 for Save the Children.

The following year I received an invitation from Lord Provost Pat Lally to recite at his first charity Burns Supper at the Thistle Hotel on 24 January. It was a prestigious event. Ruth Wishart and Brian Meek were fine speakers and Linda Ormiston sang sweetly. The address to The Haggis was my first slot followed by 'Holy Willie's Prayer'. Audiences vary and their behaviour can never be predicted, especially when the drams are being knocked back. However, I must say that the atmosphere at Provost Lally's Burns Supper was incredibly satisfying for me. There were eight hundred guests in the banqueting room. In order that the folk in the far corners could see the action there were two enormous video screens in operation. I felt more like Rod Stewart than Jamie Stuart.

I've heard people say that Robert Burns was not a man of God. How wrong can they be? Our National Bard certainly knew his Bible and studied it well. He wrote to his father in 1781 saying that he was inspired by the Seventh Chapter of Revelation, 'and God shall wipe away the tears from their eyes'. In a letter to Peter Hill in 1790 he confesses, 'God knows I am no saint: I have a whole host of follies and sins to answer for; but if I could and I believe I do it as far as I can, I would wipe away all tears from all eyes.' Robert Burns could certainly deliver a fine sermon; he would have made a guid meenister. In his poem 'Tam O'Shanter' he warns of the temptation of the demon drink and wenches wearing cutty sarks.

Without doubt, 'Tam O'Shanter' is one of Burns' masterpieces – one of the greatest narrative poems ever produced. It has everything; light and shade, beautiful images, drama, humour and above all, fast tremendous excitement. When I'm let loose with 'Tam O'Shanter' and giving it laldy I'm in my seventh heaven! Did it get a standing ovation that night? But, of course!

It's nice to get thanks when you do your wee bit for charity, but I must say I was absolutely chuffed when Save the Children invited me to be a guest of HRH The Princess Royal at a reception on board the Royal Yacht *Britannia* before the yacht's decommissioning. The Clyde-built vessel was berthed back home in Glasgow. This of course was not the first time that one of the Stuart boys had been on board. Decades later I couldn't wait to follow in my big brother's footsteps. The occasion was attended by people who had given their time and talents in aid of Save the Children. After the drinks and canapés and the formal speeches, Tony Roper, of Rab C Nesbit fame, was in great form as he did his 'turn'. Everyone was presented to the Princess and 'yours truly' was in the queue. What should I say? I took a chance and asked the Princess if she could remember a certain incident at the 75th Anniversary luncheon of Save the Children in the Hilton Hotel in 1994. I was privileged enough to be seated at the top table with her that day and was asked to say grace and to announce the sale of raffle tickets. My minister of the time bought a ticket for his wife, Linda. It was a winner and great cheers rang out when Linda went up to be congratulated by Princess Anne and to be given her prize – a handsome presentation Caithness glass decanter of malt whisky! HRH well remembered the occasion and asked, 'Jamie, did she tell the congregation?' Tom Fleming (the television and radio broadcaster) chipped in nicely, 'Well for sure, ma'am, it was a spiritual occasion.'

TWO BOOKS AND A WEDDING

IN 1993 I WAS INVITED BY Saint Andrew Press to write some Old Testament stories in my own particular style. I concentrated to a fair extent on the present day urban Scots dialect of Glasgow. However, it's a blessing that our Scots speech is fluid and certainly not lacking in variety. I therefore tried to give expression to the various dialects spoken in Scotland. Once again I got my head down and this time steeped myself in the wonderful stories of the Old Testament. I studied every translation I could find and referred to many commentaries. It was also helpful to read condensed versions and children's bibles. My friend Dr John Drane of Stirling University, whose writings about the Bible are internationally acclaimed, agreed to meet me and talk. 'I've no doubt you'll be choosing the entertaining stories like 'In The Beginning', 'Joseph', 'David and 'Goliath' and 'Jonah','he smiled. 'Correct John, yes I had decided on them.' 'Well I'll not fault you there, Jamie, but I'd strongly suggest that you include the story of 'Job'. That'll give you something to think about.' I took John Drane's advice and studied the Book of Job. It is very deep! In his book *A Beginners Guide to the Old Testament* Professor Robert Davidson comments on the book of Job. 'It has been called one of the greatest marvels and mysteries in the literature of the world. If we have any sensitivity to language, we can do no other than marvel at the Book of Job. Chapters 38–42 contain two speeches from God to Job, speeches worthy of the God who is the source of all poetry. They have seldom, if ever, been surpassed in literature.'

I felt that I could manage a beginning and an ending to my presentation but I baulked at the speeches from God to Job. They were too difficult for me to handle. So what did I do? I said a prayer. The answer came right away. I remembered that my good friend Dr Robert Stephen the Buchan poet had presented the story of Job in verse. I contacted him and he granted me permission to use the relevant verses to complete my presentation. After finishing my chapter on Job I decided to include the following stories: In The Beginning; Joseph; Gideon; Ruth; David and Goliath; Elisha; Esther; Daniel and Jonah. *Auld Testament Tales* was published in October 1993 and went into the Top Ten Bestsellers' List.

My new minister the Reverend John Hegarty wrote the book cover review: 'The fascination of a kaleidoscope attracts the attention of adult and child alike: individual pieces fall together to form an attractive pattern. The first part of the Bible, the Old Testament, is just such a kaleidoscope of word pictures – tales told and retold down through the centuries. The language can change, order can be rearranged, but the stories remain the same. From the startling colours of Joseph's coat to the poignancy of the story of Ruth, Jamie Stuart has used the language of today to make the colour of each tale sparkle afresh. His kaleidoscope produces a picture that is fascinating and compelling.'

In 1994, my younger daughter Fiona met and fell in love with Martin. He comes from Malaysia and at that time was working in Law Hospital while studying to be a surgeon. In 1995, on a glorious sunny day in July they were married in High Carntyne Church. The reception was held in the Glasgow Royal Concert Hall. Martin is now a Fellow of the Royal College of Surgeons (Glasgow), and also an FRCS (Edinburgh). He and Fiona are at present resident in Sarawak and Martin is working in Miri General hospital. I'm pleased to say, they will return next year to live in Glasgow. They have two daughters. Shona is three years old and Gillian is six months old. Just before the war my brother Jack worked as a waiter in the Mayfair Hotel in London. Every Friday night we would listen to the wireless and hear Harry Roy and his Orchestra playing from the Mayfair and picture Jack serving tables. Harry Roy married the Princess of Sarawak and composed a song in her honour 'Sarawakee, skies of blue, Sarawakee how I love you.' Earlier this year I flew to Sarawak and cuddled my own two Sarawakee Princesses, Shona and Gillian and I have dedicated this wee book to them.

Professor Robert Davidson wrote the Foreword to *Auld Testament Tales* and ended with: 'I have just one quibble. Some of my favourite stories have not been given the treatment. What about Abraham . . . Jacob . . . Moses . . . Samuel . . . Saul . . . Elijah . . . Solomon . . . Nehemiah . . .? There is a rich seam here still waiting to be mined. I hope the success of this first selection of Auld Testament stories will encourage and challenge Jamie to have another go. "Lang may his lum reek" as he continues to entertain and teach.'

It had not occurred to me that my work would be considered entertaining but that's fine. The Good Book says 'A merry heart doeth good like a medicine' (Proverbs 17:22).

When in 1997, Lesley Taylor asked me for more copy I took the hint from the Professor and produced the stories he had requested, plus Isaac and Samson. Saint Andrew Press then decided to combine the two lots of Old Testament Stories, plus the full text of *The Glasgow Gospel*. We have entitled the collection *A Glasgow Bible*. Once again the book went into the Bestsellers' List. Over 70,000 copies of the four publications have now been sold worldwide.

Do I believe that prayers are answered? Yes! I do!

On the morning of the launch of *A Glasgow Bible* I was interviewed live on the BBC television news. No matter how much one tries to prepare, live TV is a scary experience.

117

Sitting alone in a tiny studio in Queen Margaret Drive in Glasgow I was interviewed by Liz McKean from London. I couldn't help being a bit disconcerted by her opening gambit: 'Now today sees the launch of a new publication of the Bible. It's been written by Jamie Stuart who is an elder in the Church of Scotland and it appears that he has done for the Old and the New Testament what Rab C Nesbit has done for TV comedy.'

However when I read a part from my book she smiled and said she rather liked it! I had the opportunity to say that Prince Charles had been speaking the week before and had commented on the majesty of the Authorized Version of the Bible and I agreed with him. 'Yes indeed,' I said, 'the King James translation of the Bible has great majesty, dignity and lyrical beauty but it's the language of four hundred years ago and it does not always communicate clearly. Regional dialects have now become more acceptable than they were some years ago. Perhaps Sean Connery had something to do with it. In *A Glasgow Bible* the vernacular is pungent, powerful and totally accessible.'

The launch of *A Glasgow Bible* took place in Wesley Owen's shop in Buchanan Street, Glasgow on Thursday 8 May 1997 when a dozen of my friends gave dramatised readings of the various chapters.

The highlight of the morning came in one of the Joseph stories. The manager of the shop, Mary McLeod, played the scheming wife of Potiphar attempting to seduce the hapless Joseph. We had no rehearsals. One of my best pals was cast as Joseph but little did he suspect how *passionately* Mary would act! He was brave in defence!

🔱🔱🔱

AND FINALLY . . .

🔱🔱🔱

AS THE DAYS RACE ON to the new millennium, I am now in my eightieth year and I can afford to look back. What have I achieved? Have I changed anything? George Hoffman, the Great British Evangelist wrote: 'One person cannot change the world, but you can change the world for one person.'

I was speaking recently to a group of about three hundred residents of Barlinnie Prison. After my presentation one big chap came up to me. 'That wis dead brilliant wee man, by the way. So it wis! See aw they stories – the Prodigal boy and the Samaritan chap – were aw these stories right from the Bible?'

I assured him that they were all genuine Bible stories.

'Right then, wee man,' he smiled, 'Ah'm gonnae stert readin' the Bible as from now!'

He asked to have my book, and I signed it for him. I hope he remembered to pack it when he signed off from the 'Bar-L'.

The Reverend John Hegarty gave good advice one Sunday morning. He preached to the effect that life is full of ups and downs. Then he said, 'If life is good for you don't say you are lucky or fortunate, say you are blessed.'

Well for sure, I've been blessed and no mistake! I've had a long, happy and exciting life, and I'm still going strong. I had a very happy marriage. My elder daughter Elizabeth is in good spirits. She is still teaching but looks forward to retirement in a few years' time. Her daughter Kirsty was educated at Bannerman High school. She has a honours degree in archae-ology from the University of Glasgow and is currently taking a post-graduate course in information technology at Paisley University. My daughter Fiona, husband Martin and their

119

babies are well and I look forward to their return to Scotland next year.

I wish I could tell my story to my old teacher at Whitehill school.

However, just let me end by telling you about 'Daisy's Big Day'.

One of my present occupations is acting as a voluntary tour guide at the Glasgow Royal Concert Hall. It is my pleasant job to escort parties of visitors around the entire Concert Hall complex. On my first tour I led about fifty people and on arrival at the upstairs foyer I identified photographs on the wall of various conductors and soloists. Standing opposite a large portrait of the well-known British solo violinist Nigel Kennedy, I announced, 'and this of course, ladies and gentlemen, is Nigel Lawson.'

There was amusement on the faces of my group and a helpful lady whispered, 'Jamie, it's Nigel Kennedy,' whereupon a jokey gentleman commented, 'Aye, Jamie, Lawson. He was a guid fiddler too!'

As an elder in my local church, I visit the house-bound members of our congregation and recently invited an old friend of mine to take the tour. Mrs Daisy Currie, a widow living on her own was, during her time as a member of High Carntyne Parish Church , the leading soprano in our church choir for many years. At ninety-three years of age she is now rather slow and finds it difficult to walk very far . Her hearing and speech is reasonable, but her sight has all but left her. She was delighted to be invited to join the tour but wondered if the walking would be too much. I informed her that she could use one of the wheelchairs at the Concert Hall. She wasn't too keen on this suggestion until I made it clear that she could get out of the chair from time to time to show people that she was not confined to a chair.

'Well, that seems just fine, James. Can Jean come too?' she asked.

I told her that I would arrange the date with her pal Jean.

The day arrived and I picked up my two friends in a taxi and we arrived at the Concert Hall. About twenty people were waiting to take the one hour guided tour.

'Good afternoon, ladies and gentlemen , my name is Jamie Stuart and I am your tour guide for today.' At this point I enquired from my party if they had been to the Hall before and also asked where they came from. On this particular day we had a few folk from Glasgow and the rest from England, Ireland, Italy and the USA. I proceeded to lead the group from the south entrance, through the six hundred capacity exhibition hall, which doubles as the main foyer, then to the inner foyers and up the grand staircase to the Strathclyde Suite. This hall can also take six hundred patrons. The suite is used for concerts, films, conferences, weddings and the like.

We then moved into the lovely restaurant and cocktail bar and from the circle entrance into the magnificent 2500 capacity auditorium. The party was invited to take a seat and all the features of the hall were explained.

'Well now , ladies and gentlemen. Would you like to view Shirley Bassey's five-star dressing room?' I asked.

Everyone always wants to see the dressing rooms, especially the stars' double dressing room – one room for the visitors and an inner sanctum for dressing, complete with huge mirrors and grand piano. On leaving the dressing rooms we proceeded past the stage-manager's control point and finally onto the stage.

'Well, ladies and gentlemen, here we are on the stage of the Glasgow Royal Concert Hall,' I announce. 'Since we opened our doors in August 1990 we've heard many fine orchestras. As well as our own Royal Scottish National Orchestra and the City of Glasgow Philharmonic Orchestra, we have hosted famous orchestras and singers from all over the world. Recently , I'm proud to say we have been enthralled by the glorious singing of Jessye Norman and Montserrat Caballé.'

My party seem to be impressed by my spiel and I catch the eye of Mrs Currie.

'I might say, ladies and gentlemen, that Mrs Currie here was the leading soprano in High Carntyne Church for many years.'

At this point, Daisy has come out of the wheelchair and is standing on the stage with the rest of the party – she is a small lady, smartly dressed, with a neat hairstyle, blue eyes and a very alert ninety-three years 'young', although rather shaky and almost blind.

'Could I sing now, James?' she whispers to me and smiles.

I didn't hesitate. 'Ladies and gentlemen,' I intimated, 'Daisy Currie is going to favour us with a song!'

Daisy winked at me, and moved slowly forward so that she was slightly side on to the group and to the 2500 empty seats.

> *This is my lovely day*
> *This is the day I shall*
> *Remember the day I'm dying*
> *They can't take this away*
> *It will be always mine*
> *The sun and the wine*
> *The sea birds crying . . .'*

She gave out with the whole song clearly and sweetly. The lady from Chicago wiped away her tears. Daisy's audience of twenty gave her a hearty round of applause.

Returning home in the taxi, she turned to me and to Jean, 'Well, Jamie – I think this must be one of the happiest days of my life. I can now say that I've sung in the Glasgow Royal Concert Hall.'

'You certainly can,' I answered. 'And you got a big round of applause.'

As I finish off these recollections I hear that Daisy has died peacefully at a local nursing home. She was a lady to be admired.

On the Sunday after her 'performance' at the Concert Hall, our minister greeted her: 'Well, good morning Mrs Currie, and congratulations. I believe your debut at the Concert Hall was a great success.'

As she took her seat in the kirk that morning, I could almost hear her singing to herself:

> *This is my lovely day*
> *This is the day I shall*
> *Remember the day I'm dying . . .*